Basics of German Labour Law
The Employment Relationship

by

Ilona ZENKER

AF166813

ZENKER Ilona, born 1965, studied at the University of Augsburg/Germany Law including special finance- and business-administration sciences, and graduated with a P.hD. in Law.

After serving as a lawyer at court and in public service, since 1994 she is self-employed as a (founding-) executive partner of a law firm, specialised in counselling and representing private owned (international) companies as well as public corporations and trusts. From the beginning in 1994 she is permanently practising the full scale of German Labour Law. She is also Member of various Law associations and teaches her deeply profound theoretical and practical knowledge, experienced in countless cases, as a lecturer at University.

Herstellung und Verlag
BoD – Books on Demand, Norderstedt
ISBN 9 783734 740060

Basics of German Labour Law
The Employment Relationship

List of Abbreviations

AG	Aktiengesellschaft (public limited company, stock corporation)
AGG	Allgemeines Gleichbehandlungsgesetz (Act on Equal Treatment)
ArbG	Arbeitsgericht (Labour Court of first Instance)
ArbGG	Arbeitsgerichtsgesetz (Act on Court Procedure in Labour Law)
ArbNErfG	Arbeitsnehmererfindungsgesetz (Employee Invention Act)
ArbPlSchG	Arbeitsplatzschutzgesetz (Act on Protect of the Workplace)
ArbSchG	Arbeitsschutzgesetz (Occupational Safety and Health Act)
ArbZG	Arbeitsgesetz (Act on Working Time)
art.	article
AufenthG	Aufenthaltsgesetz (Act on Residence)
AÜG	Arbeitnehmerüberlassungsgesetz (Act on Commercial Temporary Work and Commercial Transfer of Employees)
BAG	Bundesarbeitsgericht (Federal Labour Court)
BBG	Bundesbeamtengesetz (Civil Service Law)
BBiG	Berufsbildungsgesetz (Occupational Training Act)
BDSG	Bundesdatenschutzgesetz (Federal Data Protection Act)
BEEG	Bundeselterngeld- und Elternzeitgesetz (Act on Parental Leave and Parental Time)
BeschFG	Beschäftigungsförderungsgesetz (Act on the Improvement of Employment Opportunities)
BetrVG	Betriebsverfassungsgesetz (Works Constitution Act)
BGB	Bürgerliches Gesetzbuch (Civil Code)
BGH	Bundesgerichtshof (Federal Court of Justice)
BUrLG	Bundesurlaubsgesetz (Federal Vacation Act)
BVerfG	Bundesverfassungsgericht (Supreme Constitutional Court)

Basics of German Labour Law
The Employment Relationship

CDU	Christliche-Demokratische Union (Christian Democratic Union)
CEEP	European Centre of Enterprises with Public Participation
CSU	Christliche-Soziale Union (Christian Social Union)
EC	European Commission
ECJ	Europäischer Gerichtshof (European Court of Justice)
ed.	edition
EEC	European Economic Community
EFZG	Entgeltfortzahlungsgesetz (Act on Continued Payment of Remuneration on Holidays and in Case of Sickness)
e.g.	exempli gratia
EGBGB	Einführungsgesetz zum bürgerlichen Gesetzbuch (Introductory Act of German Civil Code)
EU	Europäische Union (European Union)
et seq.	et sequitur
ETUC	European Trade Union Confederation
EuGH	Europäischer Gerichtshof (European Court of Justice)
GDR	Deutsche Demokratische Republik, DDR (German Democratic Repuplic)
GewO	Gewerbeordnung (Trade Regulation Act)
GG	Grundgesetz (Constitution)
GKG	Gerichtskostengesetz (Court Fees Act)
GmbH	Gesellschaft mit beschränkter Haftung (Company with limited liabilty)
HAG	Heimarbeitsgesetz (Act on Homework)
HGB	Handelsgesetzbuch (Commercial Code)
IAO	Internationale Arbeitsorganisation (International Labour Organisation)
ILO	International Labour Organisation
InsO	Insolvenzordnung (Insolvency Act)
JArbSchG	Jugendarbeitsschutzgesetz (Young Person Employment Act)
KG	Kommanditgesellschaft (Limited commercial partnership)
KSchG	Kündigungsschutzgesetz (Dismissal Protection Act or Law of Protection against Unlawful Dismissal)

Basics of German Labour Law
The Employment Relationship

LAG	Landesarbeitsgesetz (Land Labour Court)
MindArbBedG	Gesetz über Mindestarbeitsbedingungen (Act on Minimum Working Conditions)
MuSchG	Mutterschutzgesetz (Maternity Protection Act)
NachwG	Nachweisgesetz (Law of Notification of Conditions)
NGO	Non-guvernamental Organisations
no.	number
NZA	Neue Zeitschrift für Arbeits- und Sozialrecht
OHG	Offene Handelsgesellschaft (general partnership)
p.	page
para.	paragraph
RichterG	Richtergesetz (Judicary Act)
SchwbG	Schwerbehindertengesetz (Act on Disabled Persons)
SGB	Sozialgesetzbuch (Social Security Code)
SPD	Sozialdemokratische Partei Deutschlands (Social Democratic Party)
TVG	Tarifvertragsgesetz (Act on Collective Agreements)
TzBfG	Teilzeit- und Befristungsgesetz (Act on Part-Time Work and Fixed-Term Contracts)
UNICE	Industry and Employers Confederations of Europe
UWG	Gesetz gegen unlauteren Wettbewerb (Act against Unfair Competition)
Vol	volume
WRV	Weimarer Reichsverfassung (Weimar Constitution)

TABLE of CONTENTS

Foreword

Title I
General Consideration of the Individual Employment Contract

Title II
General Conditions for the Conclusion of an Individual Employment Contract

Chapter 1

Chapter 2
The Hiring Process

Title III
Legal relationship – Rights and Duties of employer and employee

Chapter 1

Chapter 4
Unlawful Reasons for Termination

I. **Transfer of the company**

II. **Business Cessation and Company Insolvency**
1.) Business Cessation
2.) Company Insolvency

III. **Basic Miltary Service**

IV. **Death of the Employer**

Title V

Chapter 1
Freedom of Contract

Chapter 2
Various Types of Individual Labour Contract

I. **Full-Time Contract for an indefinite Period**

II. **Contract for a definite Period**

III. **Contract for part-time Work**

IV. **Contract for temporary Labour**

V. **Contract for marginal Employment / Mini-jobs**

VI. **Homework / Telework**

VII. **Employment / On-Call Work**

VIII. **Job-Sharing**

Title VI
Jurisdicition

Chapter 1
System of Labour Courts

Chapter 2
Organs of Judicature

I. **Professional Judge**

II. **Lay Judge**

III. **Lawyers and other Representatives**

Basics of German Labour Law
The Employment Relationship

Chapter 3
Procedural Principles

Chapter 4
Everday Business at Court

Foreword

German law is part of a European legal system which follows the tradition of Roman law. All important legal issues are covered by extensive legislation in the form of statutes, codes and regulations.

Whereas German civil law is rooted in the Roman *'ius commune,'* the history and the development of labour law started in the industrialization era of the 19th century. Germany was the first country – after England – to pass labour laws.

Regulations concerning child labour were established in Prussia in 1839, whereby the employment of children under 9 years of age was prohibited, and children under the age of 16 were only allowed to work ten hours a day.

In 1863 the German Workers Association was founded, and the Industrial Code, which was established in 1869, was the next step towards the creation of a legal system to protect workers. From 1878 onwards, Bismarck's government passed a series of laws intended to protect the working class, such as the Health Insurance Act, Accident and Disablement Insurance and Provisions for Old Age, all of which were part of the beginnings of social security.

Since the Weimar Republic, after the end of World War I, protection against unfair dismissal has been a key element of German labour law. This was laid down in Section 84 of the Works Councils Act of 1920. In 1926 a special labour court jurisdiction was established by the Labour Courts Act and all disputes concerning labour law were decided by the labour courts and no longer by the ordinary civil courts.

Basics of German Labour Law
The Employment Relationship

All trade unions and employers` associations were dissolved during the National Socialist era, and working life was regulated by the state. The fundamental features of the Weimar regulations concerning protection against unfair dismissals were retained in Section 56 of the National Labour Act of 1934.

After the end of World War II, the newly established Federal Republic drew up the German Constitution (Grundgesetz – GG) and labour laws were developed further. The re-founded States (Länder) established the Acts on the Protection against Unfair Dismissals,which mainly reverted to the model of the Weimar Republic.

There is no general code for labour law in Germany. Employment law is based on the Constitution and various statutes, ordinances and legal provisions. It develops from rulings of the Labour Courts, especially those of the German Federal Labour Court. Employment law is a complex issue, and is not without inconsistencies.

This textbook is a concise guide of the basics of labour law and the individual employment relationship between employers and employees. It is intended for readers who are looking for a short overview and reliable information on the fundamentals of German Labour Law.

Schrobenhausen – 2014

Ilona Zenker

Title I
General Considration of the Individual Emplyment Contract
Chapter 1

I.   In General

I.1.   Conditions of an Individual Employment Contract

The individual employment contract is neither legally defined nor legally standardized. The employment contract was developed out of the service contract, codified in the German Civil Code (Bürgerliches Gesetzbuch – BGB).

This is the reason why up to the present day all legal regulations of the service contract in the German Civil Code (BGB) still apply to the individual employment contract. According to Section 611 of the German Civil Code (BGB), a service contract is in force whenever the provision of any services is owed by one party of the contracting parties. However, it must be pointed out that the service contract is different from the individual employment contract because of the greater mutual rights and duties of the parties. The reason for this is a personal dependence of the employee on the employer, concerning working time, the working place and the kind of work required of the employee.

The guiding principle of German labour law is freedom of contract, which means that the employer is free to choose with whom he wants to conclude an employment contract.

The employment contract arises from two corresponding declarations of intent by the two contracting parties, without any formal requirements. The principle of freedom of contract implicates that no special formalities are required and the contract can even be concluded by an oral statement. According to the Act of Documentation of Employment Conditions (Nachweisgesetz – NachwG), the employee has the right to claim a written documentation of the essential contents of the employment contract.

But that does not mean that the observance of the written form is required to conclude a valid labour contract. The legal restrictions on freedom of contract will be explained later.

I.2. Distinctions and other Types of Contract

The service contract must be distinguished from several other kinds of contracts.

The service contract and hence the individual employment contract is different from an "assignment" or "order" as stated in Section 662 BGB, which is free of charge. The employment contract must also be distinguished from the "contract of work and services" as stated in Section 631 of the German Civil Code (BGB), because the employee is not pledged to succeed, but only to work.

I.3. Contract Parties

a. Employees

In German Labour Law there is no statutory provision defining the notion of "employee". According to Section 84 of the Commercial Code (Handelsgesetzbuch – HGB), there is only a legal definition of the term "self-employed". A self-employed person is free to organise her / his work and to determine her / his working time.

Basics of German Labour Law
The Employment Relationship

There are different factors that indicate the status of an employee. An employee is a person who is obliged to work for an employer because of a private contract, and who is in a relationship of personal subordination. This subordination is a combination of personal subordination and economic dependence. The employee is integrated into the employer`s organisation, has to follow the directives of the employer and carries no economic risks.

The distinction between manual workers, the so called "blue-collar workers", who mainly work with their hands and do manual labour and the so-called "white-collar workers", who are employees mainly involved in brainwork, has historical origins. The distinguishing features of these two groups were laid down in the occupational classification of Section 133 paragraph 2 of the old version of the Social Security Code (Sozialgesetzbuch - SGB), which was in effect until the beginning of 2005.

The white-collar workers were better paid, had longer periods of notice and were covered by a special statutory pension system. With the advance of technological progress this classification disappeared, as it was incompatible with the principle of equal treatment (Article 3 of the German Constitution – Grundgesetz GG). Although the notion of manual workers and employees can still be found in legal texts, although the two groups are no longer treated differently.

As stated above, the factors indicating the status of an employee are numerous. We are therefore going to define the notion of the employee by describing groups of working people who are not defined as employees in terms of German labour law.

➢ Employee-like Persons

Employee-like persons are neither "self-employed" nor employees as described above. "Employee-like" persons are not covered by labour law as a whole, but only by some specific sections. The fundamental distinction between them is the "economic and personal dependence on the one group and the "independence" of the other group.

Employee-like persons are not integrated into the operational labour organisation of the employer, can freely determine their actions and their working time, have to do most of their duties themselves and perform their work - for one or more employer - for more than half of their average income, which is paid by one employer. For these reasons employee-like persons are not dependent on an employer in the same way or to the same extent as ordinary, regular employees. Therefore employee-like persons are not protected from dismissal, for example, but they can sue either in labour or industrial courts.

"Commercial agents", who are prohibited by contract to work for other companies, also belong in this category. Most of the mutual duties of the parties are mainly written down in the Commercial Code (Handelsgesetzbuch – HGB).

In the same way, "homeworkers" also belong to employee-like persons, because they work either alone or with help of family members at a place of their own choosing, and can dispose of their working time freely. Their rights are specified in the Act of Homework (Heimarbeitergesetz – HAG)

Basics of German Labour Law
The Employment Relationship

➢ **Executive Staff**

Members of the executive staff have an exceptional position. Due to their function and their authority to take decisions they should be compared to employers rather than to employees.

The legal definition of the notion "Executive Staff" is not uniform and depends on the legal context in which it is used.

The Act on Dismissal Protection (Kündigungsschutzgesetz - KSchG) defines these employees - in a different way from the Works Constitution Act (Betriebsverfassungsgesetz - BetrVG) – according to their function in the company, the legal problems connected to their position and the decisions, that they make which affect other employees of the company.

The Act of Working Time (Arbeitszeitgesetz – ArbZG) and the Works Constitution Act (Betriebsverfassungsgesetz – BetrVG) do not apply to the executive staff. The Act on Dismissal Protection (Kündigungssschutzgesetz – KSchG) only partly covers members of the executive staff. They are treated as a separate group of employees, and are not fully protected by law in the same way as regular employees.

➢ **Freelancers**

Freelancers are classified as self-employed and independent contractors. They are personally independent, create their own working conditions, are not bound to the instructions of an employer, can determine their manner and the time in which they work, and are paid according to their actual working performance. This mode of employment is mainly used in newspaper enterprises and in the food service industry. Free collaborators have no legal protection in case of illness and are not entitled to paid vacation.

This legal concept made it possible for employers to bypass the legal cancellation protection for their employees, and to avoid paying social insurance for them. The jurisdiction of the German Federal Court of Labour decided that the parties of a contract cannot define the classification of their relationship by mutual agreement in order to escape the protection of labour law and social insurance.

The assessment of the relationship determines whether the contract is classified as a labour contract or a service contract of an independent contractor and depends on the outward appearance of the relationship and not on the heading or wording of the mutual agreement. The degree of personal subordination and the economic dependency of the freelancer will finally decide on the legal status.

➢ Civil Servants

The centrepiece of the employer-employee relationship is the individual labour contract, which is a private contract according to Section 611 of the German Civil Code (Bürgerliches Gesetzbuch – BGB). Therefore career public servants are therefore excluded from the labour law, because their relationship to the state is not based on a private contract, but on civil service law (Beamtenrecht), which is part of public law. Their rights and duties are established by acts of the Federal Republic, and disputes are settled by administrative courts instead of labour courts.

According to Article 33 paragraph V of the German Constitution (Grundgesetz – GG), judges and soldiers are not defined as employees either, because their public relationship to their employer – the state – is based on an administrative act and not on a contract.

On the other hand, ordinary employees who are not civil servants but work in the public sector are covered by labour law, because their contractual relationship is based on a private individual labour contract.

b.   Employers

The employer as the counterpart and contract partner of the employee can either be a natural or individual person, or a legal person in form of a corporate body. At all events the employer has to have at least one employee.[1]

If a corporate body like, for example, a public limited company, is in the position of an employer, the legal person cannot exercise authority or issue directives, because the entity is not capable of acting. The official organ acts for the juristic person and the operating manger must always be a natural person, who then acts as an employer.

II.   Theories about the scources of the individual employment relationship.

II.1.   Integration Theory

In the past, the "theory of integration" laid down that the individual employment contract was not established by the conclusion of the labour contract alone, but rather by the integration of the employee into the organisation of the employer's company. The employer-employee relationship thus consisted of two elements, and the employment contract was considered to be the first step only, giving the employee the right to be engaged and integrated by the employer. The second step was fulfilled when the employee actually started

---

[1]   BGH NJW 1981,1270

working[2]. This legal structure was very complicated and proved to be insufficient, as the employer could refuse to integrate the employee into his enterprise and then deny him his wages.

II.2.　Contractual Theory

The contractual theory stipulates that the individual employment contract is established by the conclusion of the contract, and that the ensuing start of employment merely puts this into effect.[3]

According to the German Federal Labour Court, the contractual theory now has undisputed priority.[4]

Chapter II

Sources of German Labour Law and the Employment Relationship

I.　Law of Nations / International Law / Law of European Union

I.1.　Law of Nations

The employee-employer relationship is no longer subject to national industrial law alone, but to a mixture between supranational and national law. Only the supranational law, guaranteed by Art 24 and Art 25 of the German Constitution (Grundgesetz – GG), is valid beyond national boundaries and forms the basis of intergovernmental agreements protecting the interests of employees.

---

[2]　Nikisch, Arbeitsrecht, 1. Auflage 1951, Seite 81
[3]　BAG NZA 1998,752
[4]　BAG NZA 2002,1177

a.   International Labour Organisation (IAO)

Initially, the duty of the International Labour Organisation (IAO) – an independent specialized agency of the UNO in Geneva – was to create uniform occupational safety measures within different countries. So far, the Federal Republic of Germany has ratified only 82 of the 188 conventions of the International Labour Organisation (IAO), and the degree of direct legal influence these IAO agreements have on the relationship between employees, employers and trade unions, is still a matter of dispute.

b.   European Convention of Human Rights and European Social Charter

In contrast to the 1950 European Convention of Human Rights, which is valid in German federal law, the question of whether the agreements of the European Social Charter are legally binding in matters between German employees and German employers, is still a subject of controversy.

I.2.   International Law

A distinction must be made between the supranational law mentioned above and the "international labour law" of Germany, as stated in the introductory Act to the German Civil Code (EGBGB), which was replaced in 2008 by the clauses of Rom I-VO and Rom II – VO.

The Clauses of this law refer especially to the case of German employees working in foreign countries, and foreign employees working in Germany, and to the question of which national labour law is applicable. According to Art 3 Rom I-VO, the contract parties are basically free to determine which national law comes into force. If such an agreement is missing, as stated in Art 8 II Rom I-VO, the law of the country in which the employee predominantly works comes into force. This law is then conclusive for all aspects of the employment relationship.

I.3.   Law of the European Union

The Labour Law of the European Union comprises two parts – the primary and the secondary law. The former consists of the final form of the founding contract, ratified in Lisbon - 13.12.2007 – and its amendments and alterations, while the latter incorporates all the by-laws and regulations. The secondary law is mandatory and replaces contrary national law.

The relationship between the Labour Law of the European Union and the German Labour Law is not clear in all details. Some decisions of the European Court received widespread attention, e.g. the compatibility of national law with the prohibition of sexual discrimination.

For the European Court of Justice (Europäischer Gerichtshof - EuGH) the law of the European Union is an independent system of laws. In the case of a conflict between the Law of the European Union and the German Labour Law, the Federal Constitutional Court (Bundesverfassungsgericht – BVerfGH) – the highest court of the Federal Republic of Germany - insists on its right to prove that the dispensation of justice accords with the fundamental rights of the German Constitution (Grundgesetz GG).

The European Court of Justice (ECJ) and the German Federal Constitutional Court (BVerfGH) finally agreed that European Law has priority, but that the regulations of the German national Labour Law are not invalid, only inapplicable.

Supranational law is still very much in the background in Germany, but time will bring increased awareness of the importance of international law.

II. National Law

II.1. Hierarchy of legal sources

The legal regulations used in German labour law are not summarized in one standardized code of law. Art 30 of the Unification Treaty of the Federal Republic of Germany includes a directive to create such a book of statutes. However all attempts have failed up to now, either because of resistance from divergent lobbies or because of the lack of clear directives from the legislator. In spite of the prospect of European integration, it is very unlikely that a comprehensive codification will be achieved.

Regulations concerning individual labour law, for example, are widely scattered in over 30 separate laws, including:

➢ Constitution (Grundgesetz – GG)

➢ Civil Code (Bürgerliches Gesetzbuch – BGB)

➢ Commercial Code (Handeslgesetzbuch – HGB)

➢ Dismissal Protection Act (Kündigungsschutzgesetz – KSchG)

➢ Act on Equal Treatment (Allgemeines Gleichbehandlungsgesetz – AGG)

➢ Act of Working Time (Arbeitszeitgesetz – ArbZG)

➢ Act of Commercial Temporary Work and Commercial Transfer of Employees (Arbeitnehmerüberlassungsgesetz – AÜG)

➢ Act on the Improvement of Employment Opportunities (Beschäftigungsförderungsgesetz – BeschFG)

➢ Maternity Protection Act (Mutterschutzgesetz – MuSchG)

➢ Act on Parental Leave and Parental Time (Bundeselterngeld-und Elternzeitgesetz – BEEG)

> Federal Vacations Act (Bundesurlaubsgesetz – BurlG)
> Act on Continued Payment of Remuneration on Holidays and in Case of Sickness (Entgeltfortzahlungsgesetz – EFZG)
> Trade Regulation Act (Gewerbeordnung – GewO)
> Act on Protection of Youth Employment (Jugendarbeitsschutzgesetz – JarbSchG)
> Act on Minimum Working Conditions (Gestz über Mindestarbeitsbedingungen – MindArbBedG)
> Act of the Documentation of Employment Conditions (Nachweisgesetz – NachwG)
> Act on Disabled Persons (Schwerbehindertengesetz – SchwbG)
> Act of Part-Time Work and Fixed-Term Employment (Teilzeit- und Befristungsgesetz – TzBfG)
> Act on Homework (Heimarbeitsgesetz – HAG)
> Social Code (Sozialgesetzbuch)
> Occupational Training Act (Berufsbildungsgesetz – BBiG)

The content of an individual labour contract is only valid if the conditions of the employer-employee relationship do not violate the law. Because of the huge number of individual laws, their interrelationship is of cardinal importance. This is the reason why the German legislator has created a mandatory ranking of all laws and provisions.

II.2. Constitution

At the top of the hierarchy of legal sources is the Constitution (Grundgesetz – GG), which plays a dominant role in individual labour law.

This is because of those constitutional rights which affect industrial law directly, like the right of personality (Art 1 and 2 GG), freedom of opinion and speech (Art 5 GG), freedom of conscience and belief (Art 5 GG), freedom to choose a career (Art 12 GG) and so on. The property right (Art 14 GG) and in particular the right to own the means of production are fundamental to the free market economy, and result in the superiority of employers. Labour law, which protects the rights of the employees, is based on the Social State Principle as specified in Art 20, 28 GG, and restricts the power of employers, regardless of their economic supremacy.

The working conditions of employees on the one hand and the employer's conditions of production on the other hand are inseparably linked. This is the reason why Art 9 section III GG consistently addresses the protection and improvement of both working and economic conditions. This combination of the interests of both parties is in step with national and global economic development, and must be adjusted to fit changing political and social aims. Thus Labour law will always remain in a state of evolution.

Legal problems not regulated by the legislator, or unclear legal or general terms, must be interpreted in the light of the basic rights of the Constitution, and it is in this way that the Constitution shapes the entire legal framework, affecting all other legal rulings indirectly. This clearly strengthens the power of the Federal Constitutional Court and judicial law, and influences the development of individual labour law.

Basics of German Labour Law
The Employment Relationship

II.3.   Ordinary Legislation

Because of the large numbers of legal provisions and acts –
as described above – the level of protective legislation is
comparatively high in Germany. Laws and ordinances affect
the employment relationship. We have to distinguish between
mandatory provisions on the one hand, which are not negotiable by the contract parties, and regulations on the other
hand, which are alterable by mutual consent and are thus
negotiable.

Mandatory regulations - like the Maternity Protection Act,
Occupational Health and Safety Act, and Employment Protection Act – whose chief purpose is to protect the employees interests, are not alterable to the disadvantage of the
employee. However, the contract parties are allowed to
change the provisions in order to improve the conditions of
the employees. In this case, the contract parties raise the
level of protective rights above the legal standard. These are
so called unilateral or partial mandatory provisions.

II.4.   Court Decisions

As mentioned above, the court decisions of the Federal Constitutional Court play a very important role in labour law. According to the Act on Court Procedure in Labour Law (Arbeitsgerichtsgesetz – ArbGG), the Federal Labour Court has
the sole power to further expand labour law.

Parts of industrial law – like, for example, labour conflicts -
are not fully regulated. The need for the specification and in-
terpretation of general terms and rules, and the filling of legal gaps left open by the legislator, explain the importance
of the German Federal Labour Court and justify its leading
role.

Due to the technical, economical and social changes in the employment sector, the jurisdiction of the Federal Constitutional Court is frequently modified, and one can therefore safely say that nothing is more constant in this field than change. The employers and employees concerned have to struggle against highly unpredictable court decisions and legal uncertainty.

It must be stressed that "laws made by judges", or case law, is not an independant legal source. The binding force of the rulings of the German Federal Court must be qualified as "de facto".

The sentences that are pronounced depend on the specific facts and circumstances of each single case, and can be taken over as common or customary law in the course of time.

The question remains as to which extend the leading role of the Federal Labour Court still conforms to the principle of separation of power between the legislative and executive body, as laid down by the Constitution (Art 20.III. GG).

II.5.   Employment Contract

The function of the individual employment contract serves mainly to lay down the rights and duties of employees and employers, according to its contents. Although the employment contract is covered by, for example, protective laws, the individual employment contract, as stated in Section 611 of the German Civil Code (BGB), is the core of the employment relationship. It is basically entirely up to the parties involved to decide whether, with whom and under what conditions they conclude an employment contract. That is called freedom of contract.

This was taken to be an important improvement at the beginning of the 19th century. However, it later became evident that total freedom caused fierce competition amongst the employees, which led, in turn, to a worsening of the overall working condition. This unwanted and unfavourable development was, of course, only to the employers advantage, and resulted in restriction on the conclusion of employment contracts. The freedom of legal arrangement was further limited by several industrial safety regulations. Nevertheless, freedom of contract has survived as the basic idea and principle of individual labour law.

This is the unassailable rule concerning labour contracts with private employers. If an employee is instead applying for a job in the public sector, the employee cannot require the conclusion of a labour contract in general. The public employer has only the obligation to make a decision - using equitable discretion – whether to conclude a contract with that particular candidate or not.

II.6. Collective Agreements

The rights and duties of an employment contract can also be affected by collective agreements, known as union agreements. These are contracts between trade unions on the one hand, representing employees who are union members, and employer associations on the other hand, representing their members. Collective agreements are made up of two parts – the contractual and the normative section.

The former specifes the rights and duties of the contract parties, just like a private contract. The latter stipulates the regulations concerning the conclusion, content and termination of the employment relationship.

The clauses of a collective agreement only cover those members of a labour union whose employer is himself a member of an employer's association, and who has finally signed a collective agreement. Then the union agreement is legally binding for these parties.

In certain circumstances the collective agreement can also have a direct effect on all individual employment relationships. This is the case when the collective agreement has been declared to be "generally binding" by the federal minister of employment, as laid down by Section 5 of the Act of Collective Agreement (Tarifvertragsgesetz – TVG). This declaration is a substitute for the absence of union membership on the part of an employee, or the missing membership to an employers association on the part of an employer.

Every collective agreement has a certain term, is limited to a particular geographical area and concerns a special branch in the world of work. If all these above conditions are fulfilled, the individual labour contract of an employee who is not a member of the trade union can thus be affected by such a union - or collective – agreement.

In some cases the union agreement may even fall below the minimum standards of working conditions stipulated by the legislator.

II.7. Company Agreements

Company agreements always cover the entire personnel of the company, whether they are union members or not. This work agreement is also called the "*law of the company*" and is a contract between the employer and the works council of the company. The clauses of a company agreement are as effective and as valid as a law, as stated in Section 77 para-

Basics of German Labour Law
The Employment Relationship

graph IV of the Works Constitution Act (Betriebsverfassungsgesetz – BetrVG). Because of the principle of favourability, priority is given to those clauses of the individual employment contract which are more advantageous to the employee than the company agreement regulations.[5] The relationship between collective and company agreements as well the relationship between collective agreements and court decisions are subjects for constant and heated dispute.

II.8. General Conditions and Terms

Standardized or preformulated regulations used for a wide range of individual employment contracts, regardless of the special characteristics of a particular employment relationship, can be compared to general conditions and terms, or general business terms. If such general or preformulated terms are used in an individual working contract, they are only valid if they do not violate Section 305 of the Civil Code (Bürgerliches Gesetzbuch – BGB), or the ensuing terms which have replaced the law of general terms and conditions since 1.1.2002. According to Section 307, paragraph 1, sentence 2, of the German Civil Code (BGB), the principle of transparency demands from every user of such general terms that contract partners can identify their rights and duties clearly and unmistakably. In uncertain cases violation of the rules of transparency, or unreasonable discrimination, leads to invalidity of the used terms.

---

[5]   BAG NZA 1990,351

II.9.   Custom

The regular repetition of certain behaviour – like the paying of an annual Christmas bonus, additional maternity benefit or vacation money – can become the subject of a claim by the employee, although there is no written agreement between the contract parties concerning these privileges or payments. The fact of doing something repeatedly or permanently – mostly over a certain period of time - will be integrated into the working contract, if the employer intends to establish legal relations[6] and the employee can trust the employer to continue in this manner. Paying a certain bonus or premium three times running without any reservations obliges the employer to continue payment. These privileges granted voluntarily by the employer are called "Betriebliche Übung" and cannot be simply taken away.

The exact classification is controversial. According to the prevalent social contract theory, the permanent payment of a bonus is qualified as an offer from the employer, which is accepted by the employee indirectly by receiving and keeping the payment.

The privilege or the payment is then part of the employment contract and can be changed only by mutual consent or by a dismissal with the option of altered employment conditions.

II.10.   Right to issue Instructions

The right to issue instructions gives the employer the right to specify the work expected of the employee. The employment contract usually only specifies the fundamentals of the employment relationship and not the details of the job performance. The vaguer the job description, the broader is the

---

[6]   BAG NZA 1998,423

Basics of German Labour Law
The Employment Relationship

employer's right to issue instructions. The employment contract is not only the legal basis for this right, but also sets its limits, especially if the contract includes a detailed description of the sphere of activity.[7] The fact that an employee has been assigned to a certain job for a long period of time, may lead him or her to claim for unaltered continuation, since these precise working conditions have become the content of the employment contract. This will/may limit the employer's right of instruction.

II.11.   Overview of the Ranking

The validity of the content of the employment relationship depends on a variety of factors, and because of the wide range of laws and regulations, the ranking and hierarchy of the legal sources and their relation to each other are decisive.

European Union Law

German Constitution

German Laws / mandatory

Collective Agreements / mandatory

Company Agreements / mandatory

Individual Employment Contract

General Terms and Conditions

Custom

Right to Issue Instructions

German Law / dispensable

Collective Agreements / dispensable

---

[7]   BAG NZA 1990,561

Title II

General Conditions for the Conclusion of an Individual Employment Contract

Chapter I

Every employment agreement creates an employment relationship. The individual employment contract defines the specific working conditions for the employer and the employee, such as salary, working time or working place. The term "employment relationship" refers to the entire legal relationship between the contracting parties.

I. Legal capacity

An employment contract is the result of two declarations of intent by the contracting parties – the offer and the acceptance of this offer as stated in Sections 145 and 147 German Civil Code (BGB – Bürgerliches Gesetzbuch). Full contractual capacity is an essential condition for a valid declaration of intent and hence for the valid conclusion of a contract. [8]

Persons who are legally incompetent – as laid down in Section 104 of the German Civil Code (BGB), or persons who have only limited legal capacity – as stated in Section 106 of the German Civil Code (BGB), - cannot normally conclude a valid contract or, as in this case, an individual employment contract.

---

[8] Palandt, Beck`sche Kurzkommentar, Bürgerliches Gesetzbuch, 2012, § 145, Rdr. 1 ff.

Basics of German Labour Law
The Employment Relationship

II.1.) Legal incapacity

According to Section 104 Nr. 1 BGB, all persons under the age of 7 are legally incompetent. [9]

Sections 104 Nr. 2 and Nr. 3 BGB have determined two other grounds for legal incompetence. Adults suffering from permanent mental disturbance, or persons officially placed under the control of a legal guardian on grounds of insanity, are legally incompetent.

All declarations of intent by such persons are null and void, according to Section 105 paragraph 1 of the German Civil Code (BGB). Not even the legal representative can confirm a statement of declared intent on the part of a legally incapable person.

In the case a legally capable person making a declaration of intent towards a legally incapable person, this statement becomes valid at the very moment the declaration reaches the legal representative of the legally incapable person, as laid down in Section 131 of the German Civil Code (BGB).

In accordance with Section 105 paragraph 2 of the German Civil Code (BGB), a declaration of intent is void if it is delivered to a person who is unconscious, or in a temporary state of mental disturbance, even if this person is basically legally capable.

II.2.) Limited legal capacity

Minors who are seven and over, but who have not yet reached their eighteenth birthday, are persons with limited legal capacity – as laid down in Section 106 of the German Civil Code (BGB).

---

[9] Palandt, Beck´scher Kurzkommentar, Bürgerliches Gesetzbuch, 71.Auflage, 2012, § 104 Rndr. 1 ff

Most legal transactions carried out by a person of limited legal capacity result in a provisionally ineffective contract. The transactions are only valid from the very beginning if the person with limited legal capacity has acted with the consent or permission of the legal representative, who is usually a parent of the minor. If this has been omitted, the legal transaction can be approved by the legal representative at a later date. In the meantime the legal action is only provisionally invalid.

There are some exceptions to this principle, as laid down in Sections 107 and 110 of the German Civil Code (BGB). If the declaration of intent is only of advantage to the minor, the legal action is valid right from the beginning, e.g. the acceptance of a gift which does not involve the personal commitment of the minor.

II.3. Underage Employees and Employers

Section 110 of the German Civil Code (BGB) is named "the pocket money section", and states that a contract concluded by a minor without the prior consent of his legal representative is valid from the beginning if the minor performs services in conformity with the contract and the money is given to him by the legal representative or by a third party who has been given the representative`s consent for this purpose. [10]

Another exception is written down in Section 113 of the German Civil Code, which concerns under-age employees and their limited contractual capacity as minors. Minor employees can be qualified as fully legally competent if their legal representative – usually a parent - have authorized them to

---

[10] Münchener Kommentar zum Bürgerlichen Gesetzbuch mit Nebengesetzen, 5. Aufl., 2006-2010, § 110

Basics of German Labour Law
The Employment Relationship

conclude, fulfil or terminate an employment contract. The fully legal capacity of the minor employee is limited to affairs connected with the working place and its effects.[11]

This does not apply to vocational training contracts, because, according to the Vocational Training Act (Berufsausbildungsgesetz – BBiG), this kind of contract does not qualify as an employment contract.

An under-age employer - as specified in Section 112 of the German Civil Code (BGB) – may run a business if the minor employer is authorized by his or her legal representative and by the guardianship court. The minor employer is considered to be legally competent in regard to all the affairs of the business, and is therefore also entitled to conclude employment contracts with employees.

II.   Legal prohibitions concerning the conclusion of an employment contract

1. The freedom to conclude an employment contract is restricted by certain employment prohibitions which particularly concern children and adolescents.

Child labour is defined in the Young Persons Employment Act (Jugendarbeitsschutzgesetz – JArbSchG). Under the terms of Section 2 JArbSchG, children are young people under the age of 15, and adolescents are young people above 15 and under 18.

The above law stipulates that adolescents are to be regarded as children as long as they are required to attend school. The duration of compulsory schooling depends on the laws of the individual state. This is because each federal state has

---

[11] Münchener Kommentar zum Bürgerlichen Gesetzbuch mit Nebengesetzen, 5. Aufl., 2006-2010, § 113, Rndr. 7, Schmitt

cultural sovereignty and is not treated uniformly by federal law.

Compulsory full-time education generally lasts nine school years. If a student has to repeat a year, compulsory school attendance will be automatically extended for that period.

The employment of children who are required to attend school full-time is not allowed. There are legal exceptions, as for example in the case of easy work for children aged 13 or older. Children over 13 and under 15 are allowed to work two hours a day on weekdays, provided the work is suitable for their age group and is not performed before or during their school lessons. Such tasks could be, for example, working as a paperboy, babysitting, running errands, walking dogs or tutoring schoolmates.

Children between 15 and 18 who are still of compulsory school age, may work for a maximum of four weeks per year during the school holidays.

Work experience placements in companies, undertaken by pupils during their last year at secondary school, are a kind of traineeship, and are not covered by the Young Persons Employment Act (Jugendarbeitsschutzgesetz – JArbSchG).

2. Regulations concerning employment prohibitions and restrictions are also stated in the Social Security Code (Sozialgesetzbuch – SGB).

Pursuant to Section 284 SGB III in conjunction with Section 4,18 of the Residence Act (Aufenthaltsgesetz – AufenthG), foreign workers without a work permit issued by the German Federal Employment Agency (Bundesagentur für Arbeit) may not be employed. Employers from other member countries of the EU are excluded from this ban, unless they are residents of countries that have recently become members of the EU.

Basics of German Labour Law
The Employment Relationship

3. The freedom to conclude an employment contract is not only characterized by bans and sanction – as described above – but also by legal recommendations.

Section 71,77 of the Social Security Code IX (Sozialgesetzbuch IX), obliges companies with more than 20 employees to engage severely handicapped employees up to a mandatory percentage of 5 % of their workforce. Employers can bypass this regulation by paying compensatory payment as stated in Section 77 of the Social Security Code IX (Sozialgesetzbuch IX). For each post reserved for disabled employees that remains vacant, the employer has to pay between 105.-€ and 260.- € per month and workplace.

III.   Formal requirements

III.1.   General formal provisions

The basis of every employment relationship is an employment contract, which arises from corresponding declarations of intention by the two contracting parties.

Like every other contract an employment contract can also be made informally. There are no formal requirements and the contract can be made by means of conclusive behaviour.

If an employee or employer says that "there was no employment contract", it can be taken to mean that no written contract was drawn up.

In reality, however, in most cases the parties have "de facto" entered into an employment agreement. A disadvantage of this procedure is that without any written documentation of the contents of the employment contract, a party making a legal claim may well find it extremely difficult to provide the required evidence.

If the parties conclude a temporary employment contract for a fixed term, it is only the sunset clause or time limitation that must be put down in writing. If this is omitted, the contract will be valid for an indefinite period of time (see Section 14 paragraph V and Section 21 of the Act on Part-Time Work and Fix-Term Contracts (Teilzeitbefristungsgesetz – TzBfG)). The employer has the right to raise an objection within a period of three weeks after the ending of the fixed-term contract. According to Section 16, 17 and 21 of the Act on Part-Time Work and Fix-Term Contracts (Teilzeitbefristungsgesetz – TzBfG), in this case the contract will not be prolonged and will not be automatically changed into a contract for an indefinite period.

Pursuant to Section 127 and Section 125 paragraph 2 of the German Civil Code (BGB), each of the contracting parties can make a special agreement to conclude the employment contract only in written form.

Amendments to the terms and conditions of the employment contract must be written down in order to be valid. This is called the "clause in simple written form" (einfache Schriftformklausel). Even alterations to the written form clause must be made in writing - the so-called "clause in double written form" (doppelte Schriftformklausel).

III.2. Law on the Notification of Conditions Governing an Employment Relationship – Nachweisgesetz (NachweisG)

Because an employment contract can be entered into at any time and any place, it became clear to the legislator, in the mid nineteen nineties, that the employee, for his own protection, should have a legal claim to a written documentation of the essential contents of the employment contract entered into. These considerations led to the "Law on the Notification of Conditions governing an Employment Relationship" – Nachweisgesetz (NachweisG) -.

That was an excellent way of integrating the Law of Notification of Conditions (NachwG) into the legal system, without hindering or making the informal conclusion of an employment contract more difficult.

According to the clauses of the Law of Notification of Conditions (NachwG), the employer is merely obliged to document all the essential conditions agreed on by both parties, and to give the signed paper to the employee within a month after the beginning of the employee-employer relationship.

The Law of Notification of Conditions (NachwG) defines the essential conditions of an employee-employer relationship, which are to be recorded, as follows:

-- the parties involved in the employee-employer relationship,

-- the start of the employee-employer relationship,

-- the place of work,

-- the sort of work that is due, according to the contract,

-- the remuneration for the work, to be paid by the employer,

-- the working time of the employee,

-- the amount of holiday, and

-- the terms of notice agreed on.

If, in the case of a valid contract that was originally informal, an employer contravenes his obligation – as postulated by the Law of Notification of Conditions (NachwG) - to make a written record of the above essential conditions, this does not invalidate the employment contract. The informal employment contract continues to be valid, despite the employer's offence. On the one hand, the employee can claim for a written specification of the contents of the valid informal employment contract, and this claim against the employer is actionable and enforceable before an industrial court. On the other hand, if the employer's failure to record the conditions leads to a dispute over the contents and extent of the employment contract, the employee has the benefit of some proof relief. It is then not the employee who must prove the contents and extent of the employment contract, but rather, by way of shifting the burden of proof, it is the employer who must prove that the terms of the employment contract are not those claimed by the employee.

IV. Acceptance by consensus of the employment contract

The basis of every employment relationship is an employment contract which arises from corresponding declarations of intent by the two contracting parties.

One of the contracting parties makes an offer, as in Section 145 of the German Civil Code (BGB), and declares his intent. The other party, the recipient of this declaration, then accepts the offer, as stated in Section 147 of the German Civil Code (BGB).

In order to express a valid declaration of intent, the person must be aware that he or she is entering a legal transaction ("Handlungs- und Erklärungsbewußtsein") and establishing legal relations ("Geschäftsbindungswille"). According to Section 130 paragraph 2 of the German Civil Code (BGB), it is of no consequence if the tenderer dies or becomes legally incapable after expressing a valid declaration of intent.

The declaration of intent has to reach the addressee in order to produce the desired legal effects. This is a direct consequence of Section 130 paragraph I sentence 1 of the German Civil Code (BGB), which stipulates that a declaration of will has to come into the possession either of the addressee or of a third party entitled to accept the declaration. Thereby, in ordinary circumstances, the addressee must have the opportunity to take note of the declaration of intent.

The content of the offer must be expressed clearly, so that the mere acceptance of the offer validates the contract.

The recipient must state his declaration of acceptance within a required period of time, and this statement must be received by the tenderer. According to Section 147 of the German Civil Code (BGB), the length of this period depends on whether the persons receiving the declaration of intent are present or not. If the declaration of acceptance is adopted at a later date, it qualifies as a new offer, as stated in Section 150 paragraph 1 of the German Civil Code (BGB).

Pursuant to Section 150 paragraph 2 of the German Civil Code (BGB), the same applies if the offer is only accepted in a modified version.

V. Power of attorney and proxy

V.1. Authority of attorney and proxy

An employer concluding an employment contract can be either a natural or a legal person. In the first case, the employer himself bears all rights and responsibilities concerning the employment relationship. In the latter case, the burden lies with the person representing the legal entity, and it is this person who could incur liabilities.

The shareholders of a general partnership ("Offene Handelsgesellschaft – OHG) or of a limited commercial partnership (Kommanditgesellschaft – KG) represent the company, and their authority is required by law.

The company members, according to Section 125 paragraph 1 of the Commercial Code (Handelsgesetzbuch – HGB), usually have the sole right to represent the company legally and hence the right to conclude or to terminate employment contracts. In the case of joint power of representation, all shareholders must act together to incur liability, as stated in Section 125 paragraph 2 of the Commercial Code (Handelsgesetzbuch – HGB).

Members of a company constituted under civil law (Gesellschaft Bürgerlichen Rechts) can only represent the company as a joint proxy as laid down in Section 714 and 709 of the German Civil Code (BGB).

General partnerships ("Offene Handelsgesellschaft – OHG), for example, and limited commercial partnerships (Kommanditgesellschaft – KG), can be represented by proxies. These can be procurators, as stated in Section 48 of the Commercial Code (Handelsgesetzbuch – HGB) in conjuction with Section 164 of the German Civil Code (BGB), or authorised agents, as stated in Section 54 of the Commercial Code

(Handelsgesetzbuch – HGB). In this case the proxy represents the company by power of attorney and not by law.

V.2.   Representation with power of attorney

Within the internal relationship - between principal and proxy – it must be clearly distinguished whether or not there is in fact a proper power of attorney. Basically, no particular form is required when giving authority to a proxy, as stated in Section 167 paragraph 2 of the German Civil Code (BGB). The principal is free to determine the level of the power of attorney.

The revelation of that power of attorney of a proxy in relation to third parties while acting for the principle is a different matter.

Section 174 of the German Civil Code (BGB) refers to the situation when a proxy has to announce the termination of an employment contract. Because a letter of dismissal has to announce clearly and unambiguously who, or on whose behalf, a cancellation is being declared, means that a representative always has to be explicit. However, these requirements may be moderated in practice. A phrase like "p.p." or "per pro" - meaning "on behalf of" – next to the signature is usually acceptable.

Furthermore, the representative has to add the original power of attorney to the declaration of cancellation. If a representative fails to attach the certificate of authority, the addressee has the right to reject the cancellation immediately on these grounds. The declared cancellation then becomes invalid from the beginning, as laid down in Sec. 174 sent. 1 of the German Civil Code (BGB).

There is only one case in which it is unnecessary to attach an original certificate of authority, pursuant to Sec. 174 sent. 2 of the German Civil Code (BGB), and that is if the principal has informed the addressee expressly or conclusively about the power of attorney before the cancellation was declared. This may be understood as a case of ostensible or tolerance authority. However, it is never sufficient if the representative alone informs the addressee about the declaration of cancellation.

The special regulation of Sec. 174 sent. 2 of the German Civil Code (BGB) usually applies, for example, if the representative of the employer's company has a position which automatically allows him to conclude or cancel employment contracts. A procurator, for example, a general agent or a manager of the personnel department has power of attorney by reason of his or her individual position in a company.

The question as to whether the head of a business department, a branch manager or a simple personnel assistant is automatically endowed with the authority to declare a cancellation pursuant to Sec. 174 sent. 2 of the German Civil Code (BGB), is still a matter of juristical dispute, and has not yet been finally decided by either a German State Labour Court or the German Federal Labour Court.

It must be emphasized that the duty to attach the certificate of authority only applies to chosen representatives, but not to so-called legal or administrative representatives.

These could be, for example, the managing directors of a limited liability company (GmbH) or the members of the executive board of a stock corporation (AG). In such cases the power of attorney is a consequence of the corporate position of the representative, and the publication of his or her name in the commercial register.

V.3. Representation without power of attorney

If an alleged representative does not de facto have power of attorney, it is a different situation than if a representative has only forgotten to show the relevant certificate of authority, as stated in Sec. 174 of the German Civil Law (BGB). The power of attorney of a representative who is only authorised to act collectively with other representatives is also invalid.

In the practical business world, it is customary for the members of the board of representatives to delegate a *sub-power* of attorney to each member of the board, with individual power of representation.

Taken literally, this means that all the members of the board of representatives delegate a single *sub-power* board. This does not come under Sec. 180 but under Sec. 174 sent. 1 of the German Civil Code.

As a consequence, if the addressee is not sure whether a proper power of attorney really exists, or whether the representative has only forgotten to hand over the certificate of authority, he would be advised to lodge a complaint on both counts – for the absence of the power of attorney and of the certificate of authority.

Chapter II

Hiring Process

I.   Job Advertisment

I.1.)   "invitatio ad offerendum"

A job advertisement given out by an employer does not qualify as an offer to an employee to conclude an employment contract with an appointee. It is only a so-called "invitatio ad offerendum". [12]

A job advertisement is merely an invitation to employees seeking work to offer their work capacity to this employer within the framework of the advertisement. After the applicant has responded to the advertisement, it is up to the employer to choose whether to conclude a contract or not. If the job advertisement were taken to be an offer on the part of the employer, any applicant could conclude an employment contract simply by accepting it.

I.2.)   General Equal Treatment Act

The job offer must be in accordance with the principle of Equal Treatment granted under the General Act on Equal Treatment (Allgemeines Gleichbehandlungsgesetz – AGG).

The intention of the legislator was to ban discrimination on the grounds of religion, belief, disability, age and sexual orientation. The directives of the European Union, 2000/78 EG, 2000/43/EG, 2004/113/EG and 2006/54/EG have been integrated into German law. Before the General Act on Equal Treatment (Allgemeines Gleichbehandlungsgesetz – AGG) came into force on August 18th 2006, German law had already prohibited discrimination

---

[12] Palandt, 71. Auflage, 2012, § 145, Rndr.

in several single rulings. Section 611 a of the German Civil Code (Bürgerliches Gesetzbuch – BGB) banned discrimination based on sex. Applicants applying for a job in public service already had the right to equal treatment as stated in Article 33 of the German Constitution (Grundgesetz – GG) according to their personal talents, qualifications and professional achievements.

a.) According to Section 1 AGG, employed persons may not be discriminated on grounds of race, ethnic origin, sex, religious beliefs, disability, age or sexual orientation. Under the terms of Section 5 and 8 AGG there are two exceptions from this legal rule which justify unequal treatment. Discrimination against an applicant will be lawful if the difference in treatment is based on crucial requirements for carrying out the work in hand. However, this exception must be interpreted restrictively. Even for the job as a equal opportunities officer no particular sex is required.[13] As stated in Section 5 AGG an unequal treatment will be further legitimate, if disadvantages, linked to any of the reasons mentioned in Section 1 AGG, are prevented or compensated by appropriate and proportionate measures.

b.) It is important to distinguish between direct and indirect discrimination. As stated in Section 3 AGG, it is a case of direct discrimination when a person is treated worse, for any of the reasons mentioned in Section 1 AGG, than another person would have been treated in a comparable situation.

---

[13] (BAG NZA 1999,371)

Basics of German Labour Law
The Employment Relationship

Section 3 paragraph 2 AGG describes indirect discrimination, which occurs if supposedly neutral provisions disadvantage a person for any of the reasons mentioned in Section 1 AGG, compared to other people in a comparable situation.

c.) Section 11 AGG stipulated that job vacancies and conditions for the access to an employment had to be in accordance with the rulings of the General Act of Equal Treatment. On the other hand, there was no mention of any sanctions in the case of non-fulfillment. Section 15 AGG then granted compensation for material and non-material damages in the case of discrimination concerning access to an employment. An applicant does not have a right to be hired or promoted – as excluded in Section 15 paragraph 6 AGG. It was therefore impossible for the General Act of Equal Treatment to create an obligation to enter into an employment contract and hence to elude the freedom of contract.

As far as discrimination during the course of the hiring process is concerned, the applicant can demand compensation for material damages, e.g. lost profit, if the employer deliberately disregards his obligation in terms of Section 15 paragraph 1 AGG.

The applicant can demand adequate compensation for non-material damages as laid down in Section 15 paragraph 2 AGG, even if the discrimination during the hiring process was not the fault of the employer. In the case of discrimination, compensation will not exceed the average wage of three months, even if the applicant would not have been hired without any violation of the General Act of Equal Treatment. The exact amount of compensation depends on the individual case and the seriousness of the offence.

According to Section 15 paragraph 4 AGG compensation must be claimed within a period of two months. It is not necessary for the rejected applicant to demand a particular amount of compensation from the employer. The legal deadline begins when the applicant receives a negative answer from the employer, and the exact end of the period must be calculated as laid down in Section 187 ff. of the German Civil Code (Bürgerliches Gesetzbuch – BGB). If the employer does not react or refuses to pay compensation, the applicant must file a suit at the Labour Court within three months.

II.   Application

II.1.   Duties of Revelation

The pre-contractual relationship between applicant and employer is a confidential relationship between the two parties. This pre-contractual relationship, based on trust, establishes certain duties for both parties, the most important of which are mutual obligations to disclose facts, the duty of care and the duty to compensate outlay.

It is the duty of the applicant to disclose all facts which are relevant for his or her future work – truthfully and without express request. A truck driver has to reveal previous convictions for traffic offences or preliminary investigations which could ban him from driving in the near future. An accountant must disclose a previous conviction for property offences. This obligation to disclose ends when the sentence is no longer registered in the Federal Central Criminal Register or in a police clearance certificate. The period that elapses before such a registration is cancelled depends on the seriousness of the offence, but it generally takes a minimum of 5 years.

The employer, on the other hand, is also legally bound to disclose circumstances which would affect the employee and his job, like, for example, impending bankruptcy or an imminent loss of the workplace. Beyond this, it is also the employer's duty to take suitable care of the application documents of the candidate, who, in turn, is bound to the non-disclosure of data concerning the employer's company. The employer only has to reimburse the expenses of the application if he has required uncustomary application documents.

II.2.   Legal consequences

If the applicant deliberately violates his or her pre-contractual duties, he or she is liable for all financial damages, being guilty of contractual negligence, also called "culpa in contrahendo," and the employer has the right to appeal against the employment contract.

III.   Job Interview

III.1. Right to ask questions

The right of privacy, as stated in Article 1 and 2 of the German Constitution (Grundgesetz – GG), limited the employers former unreserved right to ask the applicant everything he wanted to know during the interview.

Nowadays, the only questions that must be answered by the applicant are those which are directly related to the future employment relationship and which are in the employer's rightful und legitimate interest. The applicant is not obliged to answer questions which would violate his personal rights and privacy.

Furthermore, he or she has the right to answer inadmissible questions with a lie. However, all information given voluntarily by the applicant must be true.

The difference between inadmissible and admissible questions is a matter of weighing up interests. We must compare the applicant's right of privacy on the one hand, with the employer's need to know as much as possible about his prospective employee on the other hand.

According to the Federal Labour Court, it is only an incorrect answer of an applicant to an employer's valid question that can justify dismissal by the employer. Employees' right to privacy increasingly curtails the right of the employer to ask questions during a job interview.

a.) For decades, employers, carrying out recruitment negotiations, had the uncontested right to ask a female applicant whether she was pregnant or not. The interests of the potential employer were predominant and the female applicant's right to privacy was put aside. The pregancy of a female employee brings financial and organisatory disadvantages to the employer, for example when the internal operating procedure has to be reorganised to protect her health interests during the pregnancy. From the early sixties until the beginning of the nineties, the right of the employer to ask a female applicant if she was pregnant or not was seen as a lawful question, even if it was clear that the employer's only intention was to avoid employing a pregnant woman.

Since the decision of the Federal Labour Court in 1992, the question as to an existing pregnancy is now regarded as discrimination on the grounds of sex, and violates Section 7 of the General Act of Equal Treatment (Allgemeines Gleichbehandlungsgesetz – AGG).[14] It does not make any difference if the applicants are only female, or whether there are also male candidates applying for the job.

Even if the female applicant is applying for a permanent contract, and would be unable to start working because of an "employment ban" - Section 4 of the Maternity Protection Act (Mutterschutzgesetz – MuSchG) – the potential employer is not permitted to ask about a possible pregnancy. There is a statutory ban of employment for expectant mothers, if her work is connected with assembly-line work, piecework and lifting heavy goods.

If the female applicant were to answer this inadmissible question incorrrectly, there would be no negative legal consequences for her during the ensuing employment relationship.

b.) The right of employers to question applicants about physical handicaps violates their constitutional right to equal treatment, as laid down in Article 3 of the German Constitution (Grundgesetz – GG), and is regarded as discrimination on the grounds of Section 7 and 8 of the General Act of Equal Treatment (AGG). The employer is only entitled to ask about the absence of any handicaps if this is essential for the work at issue[15].

c.) As described above, the employer is only allowed to ask questions about any previous convictions on the part of the applicant if a conviction would be relevant to the work to be carried out by the future employee[16].

d.) As stated in Section 10 of the General Act of Equal Treatment (Allg. Gleichbehandlungsgesetz – AGG), the employer may legally require the candidate to state his or her age

---

[14] 1993,257 / BAG NZA 2993,848/ EuGH NZA 2001,1241
[15] BAG 1985,57 / NZA 2007,169
[16] BAG 1999,975

without discrimination only if the amount of income is dependant upon the age of the applicant.

e.) On the subject of an HIV-infection, the employer has the right to ask about an HIV-infection that has already broken out. If the applicant is only infected by the virus, the employer is entitled to ask the applicant whether the job of the infected applicant will endanger other people[17]. An HIV-infection is not classified as an illness, as stated in Section 1 of the General Act of Equal Treatment (AGG)[18].

f.) After the reunification of Germany, the highly controversial question arose as to the right of an employer - especially in the civil service - to ask an applicant about his or her former involvement with the State Security Service of the former German Democratic Republic (GDR), known as the "Stasi" in everyday language. According to BAG NZA 2003, 265, the question must be justified by a particular interest on the part of the employer[19]. This would be the case, for example, if there were a likelihood that the applicant might come in contact with his or her former victims, or with items of national security.

If a civil servant answers this question with a lie, he or she runs the risk of being punished by criminal law[20].

III.2.) Tests and medical examinations

Asking questions is only one part of the application procedure. The employer often wants to get to know the applicant better, and for this reason the future employee should make

---

[17] NZA 1988, 74
[18] EuGH NZA 2006,839
[19] BAG NZA 2003, 265
[20] BGH NJW 1999,1485

pre-employment tests and undergo medical and psychological examinations.

There are a variety of ways of reviewing the personal background and the technical skills of an applicant. Beside medical and psychological examinations, employers also request intelligence and creativity tests, assessment and graphological tests, drug screening and alcotests. The applicant has to present employers' references and bank references, and internet social networks are frequently used to get more about the applicant.

The legal admissibility of tests and examinations such as these are subject to exacting requirements. Tests for selecting personnel are only legal if the applicant is tested with regard to skills which are directly connected to the future workplace. Tests and examinations which are not workplace related and which are aimed at assessing the whole personality or the individual resilience of the applicant are inadmissible.

Legal commentators therefore demand that employers should be obliged to reveal the extent and the intent of the tests involved before they are carried out. The medical or psychological examinations of applicants, performed by fiduciary or company doctors, should only be legal if the physician is accredited and sworn to medical confidentiality.

The employer is then only informed about the overall result of the examination of the applicant, and is not entitled to know the result of individual studies and tests. The doctor is also not authorized to inform the employer about diagnoses.

In all these cases the approval of the applicant is indispensable. If the applicant is underage, the legal representatives, usually the parents, have to give their approval instead of the minor. It must be emphasised that all tests and examinations are on a voluntary basis and are not enforceable by the employer. The applicant is therefore not legally bound to consent to any tests whatsoever.

Even if the applicant agrees to a test, drug screening and alcotests are only legal if the occupation involves special risks for the applicant or for third parties, as does the job of a pilot or a truck driver, or if the employee has to handle very expensive machinery. If the employer has a reasonable suspicion that the applicant may have problems with drugs or alcohol, the employer may also require drug screening and an aloctest.

Sometimes employers use graphological reports to draw conclusions on the personality structure of the applicant from handwritten curriculum vitae. This is illegal without the express consent of the applicant. The applicant could require the destruction of the graphological report and could demand financial compensation as a consequence of the violation of his or her constitutional rights. If the applicant is applying for a job as an unskilled worker, for example, such tests are always inadmissible, because they contravene the principle of proportionality.

All applicants have the right of access to all the results of the tests and examinations, no matter whether they are accepted as an employee or not. If the applicant is turned down, he or she can refuse to allow the storage of the examination reports by the employer, can demand that the reports be destroyed, or that they be handed over to him personally.

A further way of testing an applicant is by sending him or her to an assessment centre. There the applicant's competence solving problems, his group behaviour or his ability to concentrate will be evaluated during a seminar course. The applicants are encouraged to do role playing games or to handle conflict situations. A group of applicants is observed by several assistants of the assessment centre, who evaluate their performance.

Because of the test character of an assessment centre, the applicants must consent to their participation and must be informed before attending the course about its purpose and the forseeable procedure. Otherwise it is an illegal method of testing applicants.

III.3.) Further sources of information

The submission of training certificates and employer´s references are further sources of information for the employer on his quest for more knowledge of the applicant's qualifications. The employer is legally entitled to ask the applicant's former employer about his or her behaviour and professional performance. The employer is allowed to gather information without the knowledge of the applicant or even against his or her will. However, the surrender of the complete personal file by the former employer against the will of the applicant oversteps the mark.

The applicant could then claim compensation from his former employer because of the violation of his constitutional right to privacy.

In order to obtain knowledge about the financial circumstances of an applicant, the employer may try to gain information from the credit rating agency. This company is called "Schufa" for short and collects information about all loan agreements and trade credits. The employers themselves have no legal right to request information about the applicant from the credit investigation company. The question of whether an employer is allowed to request a voluntary disclosure of this confidential information about entries in the "Schufa" files from the applicant, is highly disputed. It is generally considered inadmissible, because it means in effect that the applicant also has to reveal his or her personal circumstances and living conditions.

The right of privacy has priority over the interest of the employer to gather information about the applicant.

Even the internet, and in particular social network services, e.g. facebook or Twitter, are a popular source of information. Employees voluntarily disclose personal details about their lifestyle, which can be used legally by curious personnel managers. It is thus possible that the internet may become a kind of "job-killer".

There are no standardized recruitment procedures and tests. Hence the result and the conclusions are often not easy to understand. In 2002, the German Institute for Standardization (DIN) created a standard recruitment test (DIN 33430), which defines uniform quality criteria. Unfortunately this DIN standard has not yet become law, so it is not mandatory for the employer to use the standardized version, in spite of the fact that it would make the recruitment procedure more transparent for the applicants.

III.4.) Reimbursement of expenses and so forth

The applicant can demand a reimbursement of the interview expenses from the employer if the employer invited the applicant to the job interview und promised to repay the travelling costs.

If the employer invited the applicant without mentioning the question of compensation for outlay, the applicant can demand reimbursement according to Section 670 of the German Civil Code (BGB). The applicant can demand as much as he or she judges to have been necessary, which normally comprises travel and food expenses. If a longer journey is involved, the applicant can further demand accommodation expenses. Refundable travel costs usually refer to public means of transport.

Depending on the position offered, the applicant may also demand the refunding of a first-class ticket.

Posting a job advertisement in a newspaper does not implicate that the employer is going to reimburse the interview expenses of all applicants, in spite of having invited all interested people to apply. On closer consideration, the applicants cannot assume that an employer will reimburse all the interview expenses of an unlimited number of applicants.

If the employer wants to avoid having to refund interview expenses or to reduce his contribution to an absolute minimum, he must state this proviso when he invites the applicant to the interview.

The applicant has no right to demand compensation for the loss of remuneration from the employer he or she is applying to. But under certain circumstances the employee can claim time off work from his previous employer. As set down in Section 629 of the German Civil Code (Bürgerliches Gesetzbuch – BGB), the employee is excused from work if he or she wants, for example, to keep an appointment at the employment agency, to attend an interview with a prospective employer or to attend an assessment centre.

In addition, the employee can also demand paid leave of absence from the previous employer. However, this is only on the condition that the employer has worked under contract for an indefinite period of time, that the employment contract has already been terminated and that the employee has requested leave from his previous employer.

With reference to Section 616 of the German Civil Code (Bürgerliches Gesetzbuch – BGB), the employer only has to continue paying the employee his salary for a "not insignificant time", even if the employee needs a longer time to apply for a new job. The definition of the term "not insignificant" depends on the individual case.

Chapter III

Faults of the employment contract

I.   Causes of nullity

An employment contract may be null and void on the same grounds as all legal transactions. Basic reasons are for example legal incapacity, as specified in Section 105 of the German Civil Code (Bürgerliches Gesetzbuch – BGB) or a formal mistake.

I.1.   Section 134 of the German Civil Code (BGB)

Besides that, the employment contract may by invalid, if the content violates a prohibitive laws as laid down in Section 134 of the German Civil Code (Bürgerliches Gesetzbuch – BGB). Prohibitive laws in this context are not only every rule of law, but also clauses within union agreements or company agreements. An employment contract which, for example obliges the employee to produce counterfeited money, violates Section 146 of the German Criminal Code (Strafge-setzbuch – StGB) and is null and void. The same applies if the contracting parties agree to ignore the rulings of the Maternity Protection Act in the labour contract.

I.2.   Section 138 of the German Civil Code (BGB)

If the employment contract is immoral and contra bonos mores pursuant to Section 138 paragraph 1 of the German Civil Code (Bürgerliches Gesetzbuch – BGB), as for example when sexual intercourse is enacted on stage, the transaction is null and void.

In accordance with Section 138 paragraph 2 of the German Civil Code (Bürgerliches Gesetzbuch – BGB) the employment contract is also void in the case of profiteering.

A wage is considered to be extortionate if it is disproportionate to the work involved. The German Federal Labour Court has laid down that this is the case the wage paid to an employee is less than 2/3 of the normal wage)[21]. If this occurs, however, not the entire employment contract is null and void, but only the clauses concerning the insufficient wage, which must be replaced by the usual remuneration.

II.   Causes of rescission

The employment contract may be voidable for reasons such as error or deceit as stated in Section 119 and 123 of the German Civil Code (Bürgerliches Gesetzbuch – BGB).

---

[21] BAG NZA 2009,837

II.1.   Section 119 paragraph II of the German Civil Code (BGB)

Section 119 paragraph 2 of the German Civil Code (Bürgerliches Gesetzbuch – BGB), which refers to errors concerning the essential qualities and qualifications of an employee is of special significance in labour law.

In industrial law, such essential criteria are, for example, educational background, professional qualifications, state of health or trustworthiness, all of which must have a certain permanence in order to be defined as such.

Pregnancy, for example, is not considered as an essential qualtiy, because it is only a temporary state [22], as are illnesses for short duration [23]. The essential quality or qualification must be highly relevant to the work, the employee has to do. A previous conviction for larceny, is thus highly relevant to an appointment as a cashier. The withdrawal of a driving license is crucial for a truck driver, but not for a cashier; a pregnancy is a highly relevant to work as a female dancer or mannequin.

To summarize, it may be said that all questions an employer is allowed to ask during a job interview generally refer to what are considered to be the essential qualities or qualifications of an employee.

II.2.   Section 123 of the German Civil Code (BGB)

Pursuant to Section 123 paragraph 1 of the German Civil Code (Bürgerliches Gesetzbuch – BGB) the employment contract is voidable if the employee has deceived the employer. The deception may be an action or the omission of an action

---

[22] BAG NZA 1989,178
[23] BAG NZA 1974,1531

on the part of the employee. In this situation the employee`s obligation to disclose personal circumstances on the one hand, and the employer`s right to ask questions on the other hand, will become subjects of importance.

If the employer asks illicit questions, the employee is entitled to answer the questions with a lie. If the employer reveals the truth, he does not have the right to challenge the contract, because the employee`s deception was legitimate [24].

III.   Legal consequences

According to the rules of civil law, the nullity or rescission of a contract results in a voidance starting from the very beginning of the contract.

Benefits and performances, which were exchanged by the contracting parties up to that time, have to be returned, as stated in Section 812 of the German Civil Code (Bürgerliches Gesetzbuch – BGB).

To reverse the transaction of a purchase contract, the buyer gives the bought product back and the seller gives the money back to the purchaser.

If a labour contract is null and void from the very beginning, the question arises as to how to treat the employment contract up to the time the reason of nullity or rescission became known. In industrial law, the problem is that the work already done by the employee can not be returned to him. In industrial law the impact of the nullity or the rescission depends on whether or not the employee has already started to work before the reason of nullity is known or the reason of rescission is declared.

---

[24] BGA NZA 1993,257

If the employee has not yet started to work, the nullity of the employment relationship is effective from the very beginning and is called "ex tunc". The contracting parties could demand nothing from each other.

For the eventuality that the employee has already started to work, the legislative body created a special conception, which is called a "factual employment relationship".

The time between establishing the employment contract and the discovery of the nullity or rescission of the contract, is treated as if there had been a valid labour contract between employer and employee. The avoidance is effective from this time onwards and is called "ex nunc". The declaration of avoidance is taken to be a declaration of termination of the labour contract, and dismissal provisions do not to be taken into account.

The factual employment relationship does not apply, if the employment contract is null and void, because the contract violates a prohibitive law as stated in Section 134 of the German Civil Code (Bürgerliches Gesetzbuch – BGB) or is contra bonos mores as stated in Section 138 of the German Civil Code (Bürgerliches Gesetzbuch – BGB).

The avoidance of the contract is then effective from the very beginning, that means "ex tunc". A medical doctor working as hospital physician without an approbation[25] or an employee producing counterfeit money for his employer, would both fit into this category.

---

[25] BGA NZA 2005,1409

Title III

Legal relationship – Rights and Duties of Employer and Employee

Chapter I

A significant feature of the employment relationship is that the employee is dependent on his employer to a very high degree, both personally and financially. German labor law and the German jurisdiction compensate for this subordination by defining "duties" rather than laying down "rights" when defining the roles of both parties. The principal duty of an employee is to work, and the princicipal duty of an employer is to employ and to remunerate his employee. These duties are called the "primary or basic rights" of the employee and the employer, and are followed by several "secondary obligations".

In general, the following rule applies, that the rights of the employers mirror the duties of the employees and vice versa.

I.   The rights of the employer and the corresponding duties of the employee

I.1.   The right of the employer to organize the work – the duty of the employee to work

a.) The employer is ultimately responsible for the company, and this overall responsibility includes the obligation to organize the workplace of the employee in accordance with the German Occupational Safety and Health Act (Arbeitschutzgesetz - ArbSchG). The employer has to organize the working place in such a way as to ensure that the health and safety of the employee is protected at all times. He has also to examine the precautionary measures as regards their effectiveness, and to alter them if necessary in the interests of his employees.

b.) Corresponding to the right of the employer to organize the company and, as a consequence, the individual working place, it is also de facto his duty to provide the employee with work there. Although Section 611 BGB does not mention this explicitly, the employee is entitled to demand continuous employment from his employer.

This was not the excepted legal view in the past, but legal attitudes have changed in compliance with the German Constitution, especially with regard to human dignity and the employees right to personal development.[26] An employer can only suspend an employee under very specific circumstances, but cannot be exempted from the duty to pay him his wages.

c.) On the other hand, Section 613 BGB stipulates that the employee's main duty is to carry out his work personally, and he is not entitled to send a substitute to work in his place. It follows that if the employee cannot do his work in person because of illness, he is not obliged to provide a substitute. This is stated in Section 275 BGB and is also written into the employment contract.

I.2.   The right of the employer to issue directions – the duty of the employee to follow them

The right to issue instructions gives the employer the right to specify the work expected of the employee – as has already been said in the previous chapter – concerning working time, working place and workmanship. The employee is obliged to

---

[26] BAG GS NZA 1985,702

Basics of German Labour Law
The Employment Relationship

work under the employer's authority and control and has to obey his orders.

The employment contract is not only the legal basis of the employer's right to issue instructions, but also defines the limits of this right.[27] The problem is to determine whether the employer's instructions are within the confines of the employment contract or not. If not, the employee is not obliged to follow them. The conclusion is that the contractual duty cannot be changed by the unilateral command of the employer, only by the mutual agreement of both parties of the employment contract.

If the instructions of the employer are not covered by the employment contract, the employee is entitled to refuse to obey them without any legal consequences. The employer then has the right to issue a certain kind of dismissal, called a "dismissal with the option of altered condition of employment" (Änderungskündigung), which will be explained below.

With some specific exceptions, and according to Section 106 of the Trade Regulations Act (Gewerbeordnung – GewO), the right of the employer to issue directions can be limited by the employee's constitutional rights, even if the employer's instructions are covered by the contract. [28] This means that the employee can refuse to carry out the employer's orders if he considers the work he has to perform to be incompatible with his constitutional rights.

An order from an employer is always invalid if it is purely arbitrary, unreasonable or if it violates the law. A deterioration of working conditions can always be defined as a deviation from the working contract and is basically not covered by the employer's right to issue instructions.

---

[27] BAG NZA 1990,561
[28] BAG NZA 2005, 359

Basics of German Labour Law
The Employment Relationship

In the case of an emergency, the employers managerial authority may be extended, obliging the employee to carry out additional work beyond the limits of the employment contract, in order, for example, to avoid irreparable damage to the company,

I.3. The supervisory rights of the employer – the personal rights of the employee

The supervision of the employee's working performance and behavior by the employer undoubtedly violates the employee's personal rights, but in practice it is unavoidable.[29] The employee de facto accepts the violation of his constitutional rights when he signs the employment contract. However, this tacit consent does not include the undeclared procurement of information by third parties, for example by a private investigator, nor the total surveillance of the employee. The question as to whether the supervision of the employee is still within the framework of the statutory provisions can only be answered by weighing up all the interests of both parties.

The rules concerning the use of monitoring cameras in public places, such as department stores, parking lots and bank counters, are covered by Section 6 b of the Federal Data Protection Act (Bundesdatenschutzgesetz – BDSG). However, this legal provision is not directly applicable to the use of monitoring facilities in companies.

Hidden camera systems may only be used at the workplace in order to prevent severe criminal offences. They are only allowed on a temporary basis, and only if there are no other preventative measures available.[30] Continuous TV monitoring is regarded as a violation of the personal rights of the em-

---
[29] BAG 07.10.1987 AP BGB § 611 Persönlichkeitsrecht Nr. 15
[30] BAG 27.03.2003 AP BetrVG 1972 § 87 Überwachung Nr. 36 = NZA 2003,1193

ployee and should be used only in a careful and unobtrusive way[31], in order to prevent the employee from feeling the pressure of constant observation and evaluation. But in security sensitive areas, such as checkout areas in shops or cashpoint areas in banks, continuous supervision of the employees may be regarded as legal.

The monitoring of telephone conversations is always illegal if the employee has no reason to doubt his right to the confidentiality of the spoken word. If, however, the monitoring occurs with the previous approval of the employee, it will not constitute a violation of his constitutional rights, provided the telephone surveillance is covered by the proportionality principle. Monitoring telephone calls for educational purposes is in the interests of the employer and is therefore legitimate.[32]

The employer is entitled to control the work desks of the employees to a certain degree, like reading files which are lying open on the desk. On the other hand he is not entitled to read memos or private notes that are not immediately visible or hidden, or to examine the contents of the waste paper basket.

The employer is not allowed to monitor his employee's entire e-mail correspondance. However, he may block certain websites, may search through and filter the employees e-mail account on the company computer and filter his or her e-mail-addresses, particularly if the employer has forbidden all private use of company equipment, such as telephone, internet or computer.

---

[31] BAG 29.06.2004 AP BetrVG 1972 § 87 Überwachung Nr. 41 = NZA 2004, 1278
[32] BAG 01.04.193 AP BGB § 611 Persönlichkeitsrecht Nr. 1

Gate controls and body searches invade the employee's privacy and are only admissable when explicitly allowed by the employee.

In this case the employment contract must include an obligatory tolerance or permission of such intensive control methods but they are only permissible if they are proportionate to the situation at hand. In the majority of cases it is sufficient to open the employee's bags. Body searches are only permitted on immediate and compelling grounds.

I.4. The right of the employer to expect loyalty, and other behavioural standards

a.) The duty on the part of the employee to be loyal to his employer was long seen as the counterpart to the right of the employer to issue directions.

The jurisdiction changed this legal view. The right to issue directions gives the employer the right to specify the work expected from the employee on the basis of the employment contract, and details one of the primary obligations of the employee – the obligation to work. However, it is no longer considered necessary to append the obligation to be loyal, which is now defined as a collateral obligation. If the employee fails to follow the employer's instructions he violates his primary duty to work, which will have serious legal consequences. The breach of a collateral obligation is less severe. It is still a matter of controversy as to whether the employment relationship is purely a contractual relationship or whether the personal element should play a decisive role. The personal element of an employment relationship is of essential significance, because it creates a lasting personal relationship between employer and employee. Nowadays, the

"obligation to be loyal" is specified as a mutual consideration of interests. From the point of view of the employee, the
"duty of loyalty" means that he is mindful of the interests of
the employer. On the other hand the employer also has to
take care of the interests of his employee. The term "loyalty"
is now outdated and has been replaced by the "obligation
to consider the interests of both parties".

The more the employer can trust and rely on his employee,
the stronger is the obligation of the employee to consider the
interests of the employer.

Apart from the general obligation of loyalty, the parties, particularly those involved in ideological enterprises, are also
free to agree on a "special" obligation of loyalty, bound by
contract. These so-called "Tendenzbetriebe" are enterprises
which are not subject to employees' statutory rights, and include, for example, church organizations, political groups,
unions, or publishing houses with a particular ideology. If the
private opinion of an employee could damage the public
creditability of the ideological enterprise, it is legally possible
to limit the employee's right to freedom of expression. This
special loyalty obligation could even go so far as to affect
the personal privacy and individual lifestyle of the employee.[33]

b.) According to Section 241 paragraph 2 and Section 242
BGB, the employer can require the employee to avert damage to the employer and the enterprise. The extent of this individual responsibility finally depends of the position of the
employee in the enterprise.

c.) If an employee reports unlawful and punishable behavior
of the employer to the police or the prosecution authority,

---

[33] **BAG NZA 2001,1136**

this is called "whistle-blowing". So doing, the employee breaches not only his or her obligation of loyalty, but also his duty to avert damage from the company. The solution is – as it often is – to weigh up the interests of both parties. The employee fulfils his duty as a citizen when he reports his employer's unlawful behaviour to the police, and his behavior

must thus be considered permissible. On the other hand, the employer should be able to trust in the loyalty of his employee. According to the German Federal Labor Court, an employee who reports his employer to the police is only within the law if this measure is appropriate to the situation.[34] According to the German Federal Constitutional Court, sanctioning an employee who reports his employer to the police in the exercise of his duties as a citizen, would violate democratic principles. Civil law consequences, such as the termination of the employment contract, can only be considered if the report was made recklessly, or with full knowledge of the falsity of the accusation.[35]

According to Section 138 of the German Criminal Law (Strafgesetzbuch – StGB), it is not acceptable for the employee to report the matter to his employer in advance in order to solve the problem internally, because if the employee is aware of a criminal offence and does not report it to the appropriate authority, he will also be subject to criminal prosecution

The situation is different when an employee becomes aware of an offence by one of his fellow employees. In this case, it is the employee's duty to inform his employer in due time be-

---

[34] BAG NZA 2007, 502
[35] BVerG NZA 2001,888

fore informing the prosecution authority, especially if the employer or the company is the aggrieved party.[36]

d.) The employee is also obliged to respect certain rules of behaviour which are not set out in the employment contract and which are internal rulings of the company, which regulate the team-work and smooth the running of the company, such as rules prohibiting smoking or drinking alcohol. Such rules of behavior are – as always – limited by the employees right of privacy and personal rights.

Questions concerning the extent to which the employee will have to face sanctions if he violates primary or collateral obligations, or only rules concerning the internal organization of the company, will be discussed at a later stage.

I.5.   The right of the employer to demand confidentiality

As stated in Section 17, paragraph 1, of the German Act against Unfair Competition (Gesetz gegen Unerlaubten Wettbewerb – UWG), the betrayal of corporate secrets, such as technical know-how, lists of customers or the sources of purchased goods, is culpable. Pursuant to Section 823, paragraph 2, of the German Civil Code (BGB), the employee is liable for compensation if one or more of the following conditions apply:

The employee passes on corporate secrets to a third party for reasons of competition, for self-interest or with the intention of causing damage to the employer.

After the employment relationship has ended, the employees are required to maintain confidentiality concerning company secrets by the after-effect of the employment contract. However, this obligation should not unduly hinder the em-

---

[36] **BAG NZA 2004,427**

ployee from using the knowledge and qualifications acquired during his working life in his future professional life. This restriction would otherwise violate the civil right of the employee as stated in Article 12 of the German Constitution – the freedom to choose and practise one´s profession.

I.6. The right of the employer to prevent competition

a.) The ban on competition for commercial agents is laid down in Section 60 et seq. of the German Commercial Code (Handelsgesetzbuch – HGB). However, the jurisdiction now acknowledge that this ban cannot be applied to all employees and all employment contracts.

A general contractual ban on supplementary or secondary employment would infringe the legal provision stated in Sections 242 and 134 of the German Civil Code (BGB), and is therefore invalid. Even a contractual arrangement (Section 311 of the German Civil Code – BGB) can cause an obligation to omit working in a secondary employment.

In the absence of a contractual stipulation, the prohibition of a second employment in order to avoid competition is covered by Section 242 of the German Civil Code – the principle of good faith - because an employee should not compete with the employer in the same branch of business.[37] Employees who wish to work in a secondary employment can be required by a contractual clause to obtain the employer's prior approval. This is known as 'reservation of permission' ("Erlaubnisvorbehalt") The employer may only withhold his permission if he has reason to expect operational impairments to his company. [38]

---

[37] **BAG NZA 1991,14**
[38] **BAG NZA 2002,966**

b.) The only legal limits that apply to the question of secondary employment are elucidated in the Act of Working Hours (Arbeitszeitgesetz – ArbZG) and by the German Federal Holiday Act (Bundesurlaubsgesetz – BurlG).

c.) The regulations of the German Civil Service Law (Bundesbeamtengesetz – BBG) oblige civil servants to inform their employer or their principal of any secondary employment they pursue. Furthermore, they are not entitled to engage in any supplementary job that might in any way impede the performance of their professional duties, that might give rise to the suspicion of partiality or might undermine the trust and respect shown to their position as a civil servant.

d.) After the termination of an employment relationship, the employee is normally no longer bound by a general non-competition ban, which cannot be inferred from the employment contract in general or stated as a post-contractual duty of loyalty. [39]

However, the parties of the employment contract may come to a mutual agreement on a contractual non-competition clause after the termination of the employment contract. This clause must avoid causing undue hardship to the employee and should not prevent him from making full use of his working capacity in the future. In this particular case the regulations of the German Trade Act (Handelsgesetzbuch – HGB), Section 74, in regard to commercial clerks should apply to all employees, as stated in Section 110 and Section 6, paragraph 2, of the German Trade Regulation Act (Gewerbeordnung – GewO).

The agreement about the restraint of competition must be submitted in writing and accompanied by a certificate,

---

[39] **BAG NZA 1999, 200**

signed by the employer. Furthermore, as stated in Section 74a, paragraph 1, sentence 3, of the German Trade Act (HGB), the agreement is only valid if it does not exceed a period of two years and the employer vouchsafes to pay compensation for the restraint of competition, which is also called "waiting allowance"(Karenzentschädigung)[40]. The employee in question will receive a minimum of 50 % of his salary during this period, as stipulated in Section 74, paragraph 2, of the German Trade Act (HGB)[41]

As laid down in Section 12 of the German Vocational Training Act (Berufsbildungsgesetz – BBiG) and in the regulations of the German Trade Act (HGB) and the German Trade Regulation Act (GewO), non-competition agreements cannot be concluded with under-age employees or apprentices.

II. The duties of the employer and the corresponding rights of the employees

II.1. The duty to grant holidays

The employee's right to annual paid leave is ensured by the German Federal Holiday Act (Bundesurlaubsgesetz – BUrlG). The length of this annual holiday is, as stated in Section 3 of the German Federal Holiday Act and in accordance with Article 7 of the EU Directive 2003/88/EG, at least 24 working days each year, excluding Sundays and public holidays.

a.) Under-age employees and disabled persons are entitled to additional vacation, as stipulated in Section 19 of the German Youth Employment Protection Act (Jugendarbeitsschutzgesetz – JArbSchG), and Section 125 of the German Social Security Code / Number IX (Sozialgesetzbuch – SGB IX). The length of the annual holiday for part-time employees

---

[40] **BAG NZA 1994, 502**
[41] **BAG NZA 1995, 72**

depends on the ratio of part-time to full-time employment. [42] Collective bargaining has achieved annual holidays of 30 working days for most employees, which adds up to six weeks' annual leave.

b.) According to Section 11 of the German Federal Holiday Act, average wages are guaranteed during annual holidays. The basis for calculation is the average wage the employee has received during the last 13 weeks before the beginning of the holiday, excluding any remuneration for overtime.

As stated in Section 13, paragraph I, of the German Federal Holiday Act, deviant regulations achieved by collective bargaining are legal, and many of them include additional holiday benefits.

c.) Pursuant to Section 4 of the German Federal Holiday Act, employees receive their full leave entitlement after a probationary period of six months, irrespective of whether the employee actually worked during that time, because for example, he was off sick.[43] Following Section 9 of the German Federal Holiday Act, sick days are not counted as part of annual leave if the employee falls ill during his or her annual holiday, provided a medical certificate has been presented.

d.) The employer has the basic right to determine the dates of his employee's vacation period, but the employee is allowed to state his or her preference. This preference must be taken into account, unless precluded either by important and urgent company operations, or, as stipulated in Section 7, paragraph 1, sentence 1, of the German Federal Holiday Act, by the preferred dates of other employees who must be given priority for social reasons.

---

[42] BAG NZA 1991, 777
[43] BAG NZA 1989,362

Basics of German Labour Law
The Employment Relationship

An employee does not have the right to award himself leave, even if the employer has unlawfully denied him an annual holiday, thus violating his duties as an employer.[44] In this case, the employee, in order to enforce his rights, can sue his employer and apply for a temporary restraining order in accelerated proceedings.

e.) The purpose of annual leave is to maintain the employee's health by means of recreation. It is for this reason that the employee is not entitled to waive his right to minimum holiday entitlement[45] . This is also the reason why the annual holiday should be in one continuous period.

The employee is not obliged to spend his holiday in any particular way, but, as stated in Section 8 of the German Federal Holiday Act (BUrlG), he must avoid or respectively omit activities or work which are inconsistent with the recreational purpose of annual leave.

The legal consequences to the employee if he fails to comply to this obligation have been subject to controversy. Prior jurisdiction gave the employer the right to reclaim holiday remuneration on the grounds of "unjustified enrichment", as stated in Section 812 paragraph 1, sentence 2, of the German Civil Code (BGB).[46]

However, current jurisdiction only gives the employer the right to issue an injunction prohibiting the employee's unlawful activity during annual leave. In the event of a repeated infringement, and after issuing a warning notice, the employer is within his rights to terminate the employment contract because of unlawful conduct of the employee. On the other hand, according Section 3 of the German Federal Holiday

---

[44] BAG NZA 1994, 548
[45] BAG NZA 1990, 935
[46] BAG NZA 1988,607

Act (BUrlG), [47] the employer is not entitled to offset the statutory holiday pay with the employee's unlawful holiday earnings. The senate of the German Federal Labor Court, which is responsible for matters concerning leave, has interpreted the statutory rule to mean that the employee's entitlement to vacation expires if he has worked illegally during his leave.

f.) As mentioned above, the employee receives a compusory minimum annual leave of 24 working days a year, which is normally granted in one continuous period within the year of employment. Section 7, paragraph 3, sentences 2 and 3 of the German Federal Holiday Act (BUrlG) deal with an exception to this rule. If it is not possible to grant the employee holiday leave during the calender year, either for personal reasons directly associated with the employee or for operational reasons, the employee is authorized to take his annual leave during the first quarter of the next year. In this case, the employee's entitlement to annual leave expires on March 31st of the following year.

Even if the employee has been on sick leave during the previous and following year, he has the right to claim his annual holiday leave. In this particular case, the holiday entitlement remains in force beyond the expiry date of the end of the first quarter of the following year.

g.) It is basically illegal to offer payment ("paying-off") in lieu of the employee's holiday entitlement. As stipulated in Section 7, paragraph IV of the German Federal Holiday Act (BUrlG), this is only permissible if the employee cannot take his holiday leave because the employment contract was terminated during the calendar year. In this case, the legal

---

[47] **BAG NZA 2002,1055**

requirements concerning payment in lieu of vacation are the same as those concerning holiday leave.

The German Federal Labor Court has clarified that employees can claim payment in lieu of holiday if holiday leave could not be taken due to illness on the part of the employee. The claim still remains valid even if the employee continues to be ill after the termination of the employment contract. [48]

h.) Special types of holidays, for example are paid educational leave, unpaid leave, Sundays and bank holidays.

Paid educational leave is not granted by German Federal Labour Law, but the state law of most German states (with the exception of Bavaria, Baden-Württemberg, Saxony and Thuringia) and some union agreements provide employees with paid educational leave.

An employee may ask for unpaid leave, but cannot demand unpaid absence from work.

As stipulated in Section 9 of the German Act on Working Hours (Arbeitszeitgesetz – ArbZG), and in the German Trade Regulation Act (Gewerbeordnung – GewO), employees are basically prohibited from working on Sundays – in the period from midnight to midnight – and on public holidays. There are a variety of exemptions from the ban on working on Sundays for certain types of businesses that require more flexibility. In pursuant to Section 11 of the German Act on Working Hours (Arbeitszeitgesetz – ArbZG), employees who work on Sundays are entitled to another day of rest within a period of two weeks, and in most cases they receive an additional bonus.

Article 140 of the German Constitution (GG) prohibits employment on public holidays. Every state in Germany is enti-

---

[48] EuGH NZA 2009, 135 / BAG NZA 2009, 538

tled to declare its own public holidays, according to Article 70 et seq. of the German Constitution (Grundgesetz – GG), so the number of bank holidays differs from state to state.

Federal law has determined the following days as public holidays: German Unification Day (October 3rd), New Year's Day, Good Friday, Easter Monday, May 1st (Labour Day), Ascension Day, Whit Monday, Christmas Day (December 25th) and Boxing Day (December 26th).[49]

If the public holiday is on a weekday, the employee is entitled to the same amount of wages as he would get when working on a normal day, as stated in Section 2 of the German Continuation of Wage Payment Act (Lohnfortzahlungsgesetz EFZG), which is called the "loss-of-pay principle" (Lohnausfallprinzip).

According to Section 3 of the German Federal Holiday Act (BUrlG), if a public holiday occurs during the employee's leave, it does not count as a day of leave.

---

[49] BAG NZA 2005,882

Basics of German Labour Law
The Employment Relationship

II.2.   Duty to pay remuneration

a.)   Different types of wages

According to Section 611 of the German Civil Code (BGB), the employer's main duty is to pay remuneration for the employee's work and, as stated in Sections 107 and 108 of the German Trade Regulation Act (Gewerbeordnung GewO), the employer is obliged to calculate and to pay the net wage in euros and to hand over a wage slip to the employee.

In November 2013, a coalition agreement between the Christian Democratic Union (CDU), Christian Social Union (CSU) and the Social Democratic Party of Germany (SPD) established a minimum wage of 8,50 € per hour for all sectors, as from the 1st of January 2015.

The basic wage is remuneration without any wage subsidies, and can be specified either in the individual employment contract or in a collective agreement. Alternatively, if there is no such agreement, it is the wage which is usually paid for work of that kind.

The employee's remuneration can be determined according to time (time wage), whereby the employee is paid for the time he or she is working, regardless of how successful the work is. The parties of the employment contract can also agree on a piece rate, which distinguishes between time-related piecework (Zeitakkord) and money-related piecework (Geldakkord).

There are extra payments for special employment conditions such as travel and accommodation allowances, or in the case of difficult working conditions. Additional payments such as bonuses or premiums are wage components provided by the employer on a voluntary basis.

Even if the additional benefits are granted by the employer voluntarily, the employee acquires the right to these benefits if the employer has already paid them several times without any reservations. Once the right is established, the additional benefit is treated like a wage supplement covered by the employment contract.

b.)   Overtime

Overtime payment is payed for working time which exceeds the regular working hours, as fixed in the employment contract.

In principle the employee is not obliged to work overtime. However, in the case of an emergency, the employer can oblige the employee to work overtime without asking for his consent.

The German Working Hours Act (Arbeitszeitgesetz – ArbZG) does not contain any provisions relating to overtime work. Only Section 612 of the German Civil Code (BGB) stipulates the payment of "adequate remuneration". Every hour of overtime is to be paid at least as much as an ordinary working hour. The overtime bonus is usually about 25 per cent.

"On-call duty" (Bereitschaftsdienst) has to be paid for like ordinary working time. In this case the employees are obliged to stay at a particular place, determined by their employer, in order to work on call outside their regular working hours.

If the employee only has to be available and contactable at all times, but is free to choose his whereabouts (Ruf-bereitschaft), the on-call service is not considered to be working time, and costs the employer nothing. The employer only has to pay for the time the employee actually works after being summoned to the company.

c.)   Work on Sundays and public holidays and night work

According Section 9 of the German Working Hours Act (Ar-beitszeitgesetz – ArbZG), working on Sundays and public holidays in the period from midnight to midnight is essentially forbidden. Specific groups of employees are not covered by the ban on Sunday work, like law enforcement officers, ambulance personnel, firemen, hospital staff and shift workers. Even for these groups of employees, one Sunday per month has to be a non-working day.

Employees working on Sundays or public holidays are either entitled to another day of rest within a period of two weeks or they receive additional remuneration. Under certain conditions, parts of the wage subsidy are tax-free. This is intended to provide compensation for disrupting the employee's way of life and as an requital for social disadvantages.

The provisions concerning night work are stipulated in Section 2 and 6 in the German Act of Working Hours (ArbZG). Night work means regular working hours from 11 pm to 6 am or, in bakeries, from 10 pm to 5.00 am. Working for more than two hours within this time frame means that the the rest of the working hours count as night work too. The normal working period for night workers is 8 hours. Up to the age of 50 they are given a medical check-up at the employer's expense every three years. Employees over 50 are sent for a medical check-up every year.

The employee is entitled to switch to the day shift if night work affects his health or if he has to look after a child under 12 years of age or a dependent relative who is in need of his care.

d.)   Short time

Short time work is a temporary reduction of working hours and wages in response to an economic crisis.

As stipulated in Section 87 of the German Works Constitution Act (Betriebsverfassungsgesetz – BetrVG), short time can only be introduced by the employer with the approval of the works council. Restriction clauses in union agreements often allow the employer to introduce short time unilaterally. Otherwise the employer has to pay full wages, because he has fallen in default of acceptance, as stated in Section 615 of the German Civil Code (BGB).

The Employment Agency pays out short time allowances if the introduction of short time is used as a way to avoid terminating employment contracts during an economic crisis.

In accordance with Section 169 ff of the German Social Security Code III (Sozialgesetzbuch III – SGB III), short time benefits pay up to 60 – 67 % of the missing net wage. Short time is limited to 6 months, as stated in Section 177 of the German Social Security Code III (SGB III).

II.3.   Further duties

As already mentioned, the employer is obliged to give a reference to the employee. It is for the employee to decide whether he asks for a simple or a qualified reference.

According to the provisions of the General Act of Equal Treatment (Allgemeines Gleichhandlungsgesetz – AGG), any discrimination on grounds of race, sex, religion, belief or age are forbidden, and every employee can demand equal treatment.

Basics of German Labour Law
The Employment Relationship

Under the Employee Inventions Act (Arbeitnehmererfindungs-gesetz - ArbnErfG), an invention made by an employee during his period of employment is to be attributed to the employer, and the employee receives appropriate remuneration according to the guidelines of the Ministry of Labour (ArbNEG).

Chapter II

Payment without work

In principle, remuneration only has to be paid if the employee has performed his work as set down in the individual employment contract.

I.   Annual Holiday, Sick Leave, Maternity

The employee is entitled to continued payment of his wages during his annual paid holiday, as stated in the German Federal Holiday Act (Bundesurlaubsgesetz), during sick leave as stated in the Act on Continued Remuneration During Illness (Entgeltfortzahlungsgesetz – EFZG) and during pregnancy and maternity, according to the Maternity Protection Act (Mutterschutzgesetz – MuSchG).

II.   Employee´s Absence of Short Duration

Section 616 of the German Civil Code (BGB) guarantees the employee continued payment of remuneration if he cannot work for a "short period of time" for "personal reasons" and if the inability to work is not the employee's fault.

This provision refers to situations in which the employee cannot be expected to work, like the death of a near relative, the unexpected illness of his child, marriage, a child's First

Communion, the parents' golden wedding anniversary and so on. Two or three days within a period of six months are acceptable under this provision.

III.   Default of Acceptance of the Employer

The default in acceptance is stipulated in Section 615 of the German Civil Code (BGB) and refers to cases when the employee's offer of work is not accepted by the employer. In these cases the employer is obliged to pay remuneration, regardless of whether the employer is unable or only unwilling to accept the work of his employee.

IV.   Employer´s Risk

The last exception to the rule, that remuneration has only to be be paid if the employee has performed his work, depends on the question of who bears the business risk. The "theory of spheres" follows the principle that as the employer reaps the profit, he bears the business risk.

The obligation to pay remuneration is not binding if the employee cannot get to his place of work and offer his work perfomance at the location of the company, because it is the employee's reponsibility to travel to his workplace.

If the survival of the company is endangered the employee bears part of the business risk, because he has to accept reduced wages after the introduction of short time or, in the last resort, the termination of his employment contract.

Title IV

Modification , suspension and termination of the Individual employment contract

The end of an employment relationsship is a significant event for the employee, because his economic livelihood is affected. The German Labour Law offers various ways of terminating an individual employment contract.

An ordinary dismissal is still the most common way, although it is always possible to terminate the employment contract mutually by cancellation the contract. Other reasons could be retirement or rescission.

The death of the employer, the relocation of the company, a factory closure or company insolvency are not qualified as valid reasons for terminating an employment contract.

Chapter I

Termination by mutual consent

Some terminations occur as a result of mutual agreements between employer and employee, in compliance with the principle of freedom of contract. Such cancellations are unconditional and need only be drawn up in writing. The freedom to terminate the employment contract mutually by cancellation was long a highly controversial issue. Quite often the employer offers financial compensation, which induces the employee to sign the cancellation contract.

This compensation sum is later charged up against the unemployment benefits, which, in view of the labour market situation, often makes the pay-off worthless. The employment ends on a particular date without notice of termination, and is a legal method to circumvent the protection against unlawful dismissal.

Chapter II

Termination by extraordinary and ordinary dismissal

Extraordinary and ordinary dismissals are two ways of terminating the employment contract unilaterally.

I.)   Extraordinary dismissal

Extraordinary dismissals, according to Section 626 of the German Civil Code (BGB), are legally possible in cases which make it unacceptable for the parties to continue the employment relationship until the notice period has expired or, alternatively, the contractual date of expiration has been reached.

They typically apply in cases of serious misconduct or for other urgent reasons, and are only possible within two weeks of the moment when the employer finds out the decisive facts which justify the termination of the employment contract without notice.

As always, a dismissal is the last resort, and for this reason all the circumstances of the particular situation have to be taken into account.

The interests of both parties must be weighed up; on the one hand the interest of the employee to continue the employment relationship and on the other hand that of the employer to terminate the working relationship immediately.

Basics of German Labour Law
The Employment Relationship

An evaluation of the interests of the parties involved has to result in a poor prognosis for future unproblematic cooperation within the employment relationship.

If a dismissal is based on repeated misconduct on the part of the employee, it is necessary that he or she be given prior warning.

Examples of grave misconduct could be persistently refusing to work, claiming unfounded sick-leave, surfing the Internet for private purposes during work-time, pronouncing xenophobic or racist statements, committing an offence, or other criminal behavior such as misappropriation, fraud, larceny, criminal property damage or gross insult to the contractual partner. [50]

II.)   Ordinary dismissal

In cases of ordinary termination with notice, the employment relationship ends when the period of notice expires. Minimum terms of notice are laid down in Section 622 of the German Civil Code (BGB) and start off with four weeks for all employees. After 2 years of employment the notice period is extended to one month, after 5 years to two months, after 8 years to three months, after 10 years to four months and so on. However, this system of extending the term of notice does not start until the employee has reached the age of 25.

Special stipulations in an individual employment contract cannot reduce, but can also extend the period of notice of dismissal. In some cases, the term of notice required of the employee to terminate the contract is shorter than the term of notice the employer has to comply with.

---

[50] BAG NZA 2009, 779
BAG AP Nr. 73 - § 626 BGB
BAG AP Nr. 26 - § 6262 BGB

Pursuant to Section 623 of the German Civil Code (BGB), the notice of cancellation must be in writing, but does not have to adduce reasons.

Employees are protected by the German Civil Code and also by the provisions of the Act on Protection against unfair Dismissal (Kündiungsschutzgesetz – KSchG). This special act apllies only to enterprises employing more than ten full-time employees (not counting trainees and apprenctices) on a regular basis. Part-time workers with a regular working time of not more than 20 hours count as 0,5, and part-time employees with a regular working time of not more than 30 hours count as 0,75.

As laid down in Sections 1 and 23 of the Act on Protection against unfair Dismissal, employees must have completed a qualifying working period of six months without interruption, in order to be eligible for protection under this law. Smaller companies with a maximum of ten employees are exempted from the Act on Protection against unfair Dismissal.

The declaration of an ordinary termination must be socially justified and compatible. In case the Dismissal Protection Act applies there are only three justifications for dismissal which meet this criterium: Dismissal on grounds of personal capability, dismissal on grounds of conduct and termination for operational reasons.

II.1.) Dismissal on grounds of personal capability:

This kind of termination is relevant in a situation in which the employee is unable zu fulfil the requirements of his job. It is most frequently used in connection with illness, whether highly recurrent short-term disorders, chronic disease or a protracted or long-term illness.

The Labour Court has to weigh up the competing interests of the contracting parties, such as the economic impact on the company and on work performance, the consequences for the other employees, the length of the sickness, the duration of the employment relationship, the practicability of transferring the employee to an other workplace, the size of the company and so forth.

A valid dismissal on grounds of illness requires a negative or an unfavourable medical prognosis and a situation in which the employer can no longer be expected to accept the consequences of further periods of frequent sick leave. Large companies are expected to cope with this problem more easily than smaller enterprises.

The future development of a disease is difficult to predict, except possibly by the employee. Hence the employee bears the burden of proof that he will not be sick in the future. If the employee is able to prove that he has a positive or a favourable medical prognosis, it is for the employer to prove the contrary.

II.2.) Dismissal on grounds of conduct

This termination applies to misconduct on the part of the employee, and is generally invalid without prior warning. The reasons justifying ordinary dismissal on grounds of behaviour differ from those justifying an extraordinary dismissal as regards the gravity and intensity of misconduct. Such reasons might be, for example, unauthorized leave-taking, absenteeism, or the consumption of drugs or alcohol on company premises. [51]

---

[51] BAG NZA 2004,784 and 1380; BAG NZA 2006, 98; BAG NZA 1990, 433; BAG NZA 1995, 517

The line between dismissal on grounds of personal capabilty and dismissal on grounds of conduct is often fluid and a little bit blurred. Conduct refers to individual acts commited by the employee, whereas capability and competence of an employee is associated with certain personal characteristics and skills, and are mostly unintentional.

II.3.) Termination for operational reasons

A dismissal for economic or operational reasons can be caused by an economic crisis, the introduction of new technologies, rationalization measures etc. The dismissal is justified if the economic situation has made it impossible for the employer to retain the employee any longer. Redundancy is lawful only if justified by urgent operational necessities.

The employer bears the burden of proof concering the details of the economic situation and the necessity of the dismissal. The option of reorganizing the company instead of giving notice to the employee is not subject to judical control and is considered to be a managerial decision. The Labour Court can only intervene if the the employer acts arbitrarily.[52]

A futher aspect is the necessity to select employees to be dismissed. Criteria for selecting those employees in compliance with Section 1 paragraph III of the Act of Protection against Unfair Dismissals (KschG – Kündiungsschutzgesetz) are, for example, the duration of the employment relationship, the age of the employee, his marital status, number of children, financial obligations towards family members or severe disabilties. Employees who are of particular importance to the enterprise because of their knowledge, work perfor-

---

[52] **BAG NZA 1996,1145**

mance and professional skills, can be ignored in the selection process. The employee who would suffer most from the consequences of the dismissal must be the last to be dismissed.

III.) Special Case - Dismissal with the option of altered conditions of employement

The dismissal for alteration the employment contract is a genuine dismissal, and can be accepted, refused or accepted only under reserve by the employee.

This kind of dismissal is used by the employer to effectuate changes in the working conditions which the employee does not agree to. It is a regular dismissal combined with an offer to continue the employment relationship under new or changed conditions, according to Section 158 of the German Civil Code (BGB).

The employer's managerial authority also entitles him to change working conditions. In this case, dismissal with the option of altered conditions is not applicable. This distinction is often very difficult to determine, and depends on the kind of working conditions that are going to be changed. The more of the basic principles of the employment contract the employer intends to change, the more it is necessary to terminate the contract instead of using managerial authority.

If the employee accepts the new working conditions, the former employment contract and its condtions are terminated, and the new working conditions, usually with lower standards, take effect.

If an employee refuses the new offer, he risks loosing his job. In this case, Section 2 of the Employment Protection Act (Kündigungsschutzgesetz KSchG) offers the employee certain protection. The employee can accept the offer and announce a reservation at the same time.

The Labour Court must decide whether the the employer's dismissal with the option of altered conditons was justified or not. If the dismissal is unjustified, the former employment contract is still valid and the employee is reinstated in his former working place with all its benefits. If not, the new working conditions apply. Either way, the working relationship continues and the employee does not lose his job and his livelihood.

Chapter III

Other Grounds for Terminating the Employment Contract

I.   **Rescission of Contract**

As explained in Title II /Chapter III, an employment contract may be voidable for reasons such as error or deceit. This is stated in Sections 119 and 123 of the German Civil Code (Bürgerliches Gesetzbuch – BGB).

II.   **Expiry of a period**

Any fixed-term contract must be consistent with the German Act on Part-Time Work and Fixed-Term Employment (Teilzeitbefristungsgesetz TzBfG).

As laid down in Section 3 paragraph 1, the duration of fixed-term contracts must be linked with objective conditions such a particular date of expiry, the finishing of a specific task or the occurrence of a certain event.

Fixed-term contracts that have no objective grounds are limited to a maximum of two years. Section 14 paragraph 4 of the German Act of Part-Time Work and Fixed-Term Employment Contracts provides a list of objective reasons as a guideline.

While the employment contract, including the grounds for the limitation, can be concluded either in writing or verbally, the limitation itself is only valid if it is written down. If not, the employment contract, according to Section 16, is automatically concluded for an indefinite period of time. A written version of the limitation cannot be added later.[53]

As laid down in Section 14, paragraph 3 of the Act of Part-Time Work and Fixed-Term Employment and according to Section 196 of the German Social Code III, if the employee is over 52 years old and has been unemployed for 4 consecutive months before concluding the fixed-term contract, the parties involved are entitled to conclude an employment contract for a definite period of 5 years without any objective reasons.

III.   Death of the Employee

Persuant to Sections 611, 673,675 of the German Civil Code (BGB), the employee`s chief task is to carry out the work in person, and he is not allowed to provide a substitute. Hence the death of the employee terminates the employment relationship.

IV.   Voluntary Service in the Army

If the employee volunteers for a particular campaign in the German army and stays on after it has finished, or if the military exercise lasts longer than 4 months, the employment contract can be legally terminated.

---

[53] BAG NZA 2005,575

V.   Reaching the age limit

According to Section 36 of the German Social Code VI, the statutory retirement age is 67, provided that certain conditions are fullfilled, such as 35 years' membership in the statutory pension system. Persuant to Section 77 of the German Social Code VI, should the retirement pension be claimed prematurely, for example at the age of 63, the pension is reduced by 0,3 % a month for each month of premature retirement. The maximum reduction of an early pension is 14,4 %.

Until 1991, the statutory retirement age was 65 for men and 60 for women. The law was changed In 1992, and the age limit equalized for men and women. Employees born in 1965 and later will not receive their retirement payment before the age of 67.

According to Section 41 of the German Social Code VI, reaching the age limit is not a legitimate reason for dismissing an employee on personal grounds.

However, individual agreements between the contracting parties are frequently made. In these cases, the employment relationship expires automatically when the employee is entitled to claim his old-age pension.[54] These individual agreements are only valid if they are concluded within three years of attaining retirement age.

For security reasons, special provisions apply to employees in the aviation branch. Pilots and aviators reach retirement age at the beginning of the month of their 60th birthday.[55]

---

[54] NZA 2008,1302
[55] BAG NZA 2004,1352

Persuant to the Act of Part-time Retirement, the contracting parties of the employment relationship agree to reduce the working time to half of the previous weekly working hours.

However, the "block model" is more popular today than the above mentioned. In this model, semi-retirement is divided into two parts: the working period and so-called gardening leave. During the working period the employee works full-time, and during his "gardening leave" he receives his former full-time pay without actually working.

Whereas this form of partial retirement can also be qualified as part-time work, it is reimbursed by the Federal Employment Agency, as laid down in Section 3 paragraph 1 of the German Act of Part-time Retirement.

Chapter IV

Unlawful Reasons for Termination

I.   Transfer of the Company

In cases where a company is transferred by legal transaction (as stated in Section 613a of the German Civil Code (BGB), the employment relationships are also transferred to the new owner of the entreprise (the transferee).

Any dismissals based on the transfer of a company or parts of an company are null and void. The employment relationssship continues with the new owner and all the rights and duties arising from the former employment contract are transferred to and guaranteed by him.

A company has been transferred if the transferee continues the business while preserving its economic identity.[56]

---

[56] BAG, NZA 2004,845

Basics of German Labour Law
The Employment Relationship

The Federal Labour Court has developed certain criteria to define a company transfer. [57]

The material assets of the company such as factory buildings and movable equipment must be transferred, as well as immaterial assets like goodwill, know-how or patents. The take-over of the workforce and the acquisition of the customer base also play a decisive role, as well as the similarity of the activity of the enterprise before and after the transfer. Another important factor is whether the company's business activities will be interrupted after the transfer of the_company, and if so, for how long. The new owner must keep the enterprise going, acting on his own behalf and at his own expense.

Depending on the type of company involved, some factors may be more decisive than others.

Both the former employer and the transferee have to inform all employees who are affected by the transfer about the proposed date of transfer and the reasons behind it, and also about the economic, legal and social implications for those employees. This information has be given in text form, as stated in Section 126b and Section 125 of the German Civil Code (BGB).

In accordance with Section 613a of the German Civil Code (BGB) and Article 2 paragraph 1 of the German Constitution (Grundgesetz GG), all employees whose employment contracts are to be transferred, have the right to resist the transfer and demand that they continue to be employed by the former owner. After a comprehensive briefing, either by the transferor or the transferee or both, the employees have four weeks in which they may refuse the transfer.

---

[57] EuGH NJW 1999,1697 / BAG NZA 2003,1385

In this particular case, the employment contract continues with the transferor. He is now entitled to terminate the working contract for operational reasons, persuant to Section 1 paragraph 2 sentence 1 of the Employment Protection Act (Kündigungsschutzgesetz KSchG).

II.   Business Cessation and Company Insolvency

II.1.)   Business Cessation

Business cessation does not generally justify the termination of an employment contract. However, depending on the details of the case, the employer may have the right to terminate the employment contract for operational reasons.

II.2.)   Company Insolvency

The employer can terminate the employment contract for operational reasons before filing for bankruptcy. Thereafter, however, insolvency is no longer a legal reason for the offical insolvency receiver to terminate the employment contract by an extraordinary or ordinary dismissal. Insolvency does not exempt any of the parties from complying with the rulings of ther German Labour Law.

According to Section 108 of the German Insolvency Code, when an application has been made to open insolvency proceedings the offical insolvency receiver adopts all the rights and duties of the employer. According to Section 113 of the German Insolvency Code (Insolvenzgesetz – InsO), the receiver is only entitled to terminate the contract, with a three months period of notice, in cases where there are legitimate reasons for terminating the employment contract.

III.   Basic Military Service

Whereas voluntary service in the German army on the part of an employee can be a reason for termination, standard military conscription only leads to a suspension of the employment relationship. This also applies to annual active duty training, as stated in Section 1 of the German Act on the protection of the workplace (Arbeitsplatzschutzgesetz – ArbPlSchG).

IV.   Death of the Employer

The decease of the employer does not constitute a legal reason for terminating an employment contract. As stated in Section 1922, 1967 of the German Civil Code (BGB), the heirs assume the rights and obligations related to the employment contract. The employer status is inheritable.

However, if the work performance of the employee is adapted to fit the needs of the employer and is of a very personal nature – such as that of a nurse or a private teacher – the working contract will end with the death of the employer.

Title V

Chapter I

Freedom of Contract

Basically it is up to the parties themselves to decide with whom and under what conditions they wish to conclude an employment contract. This is called 'the freedom to conclude a contract' on the one hand and 'the freedom to draft a content of a contract' on the other hand.

This was held to be an important improvement at the beginning of the 19th century. However, it became apparent that this freedom caused such fierce competition among the employees that the overall working conditions worsened, which was only to the employers' advantage. This was an unwelcome and unfavourable development, and it led to several constraints on the conclusion of employment contracts. In particular the freedom to draft the content of a contract was limited by several industrial safety regulations. Nevertheless, freedom of contract has survived as the main idea and principle of individual labour law.

This is the incontrovertible rule concerning labour contracts with private employers. Even if an employee is seeking employment from a employer in the public sector, the employee cannot normally insist on the conclusion of a labour contract. The public sector employer is also bound by the freedom of contract and is thus obliged to make a decision - in all good conscience – as to whether to conclude a contract with that particular appointee or not.

Chapter II

Various Types of Individual Labour Contract

I.   Full-Time Contract for an indefinite Period

A full-time (open-ended) contract is the standard labour contract. Employees prefer the security of a labour contract for an indefinite period. This is because German Labour law places an employee in a very strong position, in particular as regards unfair dismissal.

Even when the economy is booming every employee has to meet the requirements of a probationary period, usually lasting 6 months, in order to get a full-time labour contract for an indefinite period of time. Nowadays, in times of economic downturn, most employees are only offered a fixed-term labour contract, even if they have completed their probation time successfully. It should be emphasized that employees nowadays are given the option of a lifelong position in a company much later than in previous times.

II.   Contract for a definite Period

According to the Act on Part-time Work and Fixed-Term Contracts (Gesetz über Teilzeitarbeit und befristete Arbeitsverträge – TzBfG) from 2001, a fixed-term contract is given either if the parties agree on a termination or finish date, or if the date of expiry depends on the purpose or nature of the work.

The basic rule is laid down in Section 14 paragraph I TzBfG. The conclusion of a fixed-term contract is only valid if there is a reason which justifies the limitation.

The text of the law provides several legal reasons, but the enumeration is not exhaustive. Acceptable and justifying reasons could be, for example, a temporary demand for work in the company, the necessity to replace a former employee, to test a new employee, or if the employee is payed by a public budgetary fund.

Section 14 paragraph II TzBfG is the first exception to the principle of the foregoing rule of Section 14 paragraph I TzBfG. In this case, a fixed-term contract is valid without any justification if it is concluded for a maximum period of two years. A contract for a shorter term could be prolonged up to three times until the same maximum period has been reached.

For start-up companies, the maximum duration of such contracts can be extended from two years to four years without any justification. This regulation is intended to help newcomers establish themseves on the market without too much financial liability to their employees.

The conclusion of a fixed-term contract is always invalid if the employee has worked for the same employer before. The length of time that has lapsed since the previous employment is completely irrelevant.

If an employee is more than 52 years old and has been unemployed for more than four months – according to Section 14 paragraph 3 TzBfG - the conclusion of a contract for a fixed period of five years is valid without any objective reason to justify this time limit. If the contract has not been concluded for five years from the beginning, the employement contract can be prolonged repeatedly for a maximum of five years.

Section 4 TzBfG guarantees the principle of equal treatment of employees with fixed-term contracts and employees with contracts for an indefinite period of time. Section 17 and 18 TzBfG obliges the employer to inform employees with fixed-

Basics of German Labour Law
The Employment Relationship

term contracts about vacancies in the company, in order to give them the chance of a permanent position and to strengthen their rights of information.

For the non-teaching staff at universities and colleges and for employees of large academic research facilities there are special provisions, such as the "Wissenschaftszeitvertrags-gesetz", which dates back to 2007.

An valid fixed-term contract ends, without notice or prior declaration, on the date of expiry agreed on by the parties. The employee is not entitled to claim on the basis of the Un-fair Dismissal Protection Act (Kündigungsschutzgesetz – KSchG) or any other legal provisions of German Labour Law which normally protect employees against dismissal by the employer.

If the duration of a fixed-term contract depends on the type, purpose or nature of the work – according to Section 14 paragraph II TzBfG - the date of expiry cannot be determined in advance on a particular date, because the final deadline is usually unforseeable. Section 15 paragraph 2 TzBfG stipulates that the contract expires the moment the purpose of the contract has been fulfilled. The employer has to inform the employee of the forthcoming termination in a written state-ment at the earliest possible date, at least two weeks before the completion of the project or the purpose will be reached.

According to Section 15 paragraph 3 TzBfG, the employer on-ly has the right to terminate a fixed-term contract by ordinary dismissal if the parties in the employment contract have agreed upon this eventuality in the provisions of the con-tract.

If the employment relationship continues after the expiry date, with the knowledge and consent of the employer, the labour contract is regarded as a contract concluded for an indefinite period of time.

The legal consequences of concluding an invalid fixed-term contract are laid out in Section 16 TzBfG. In this case the contract is regarded as an unlimited contract, and can only be cancelled in accordance with the legal rules for an ordinary or extraordinary dismissal pursuant Section §§ 620 ff. BGB and § 1 ff. KSchG.

If an employee claims that the limitation of the employment contract is invalid, the employee has to bring an action to the Labour Court within three weeks after the expiry date of the contract.

If the limitation is invalid because the labour contract was not drawn up in writing, the contract can be terminated even before the agreed time of expiry.

III.   Contract for part-time Work

Employees whose regular weekly working time is shorter than the working time of a comparable full-time employee, are working part-time.

The employees, which are compared with part-time employees are all the full-time employees working for the same company under the same or similar conditions.

Part-time agreements have become increasingly important during the last few years.

It is mainly female employees who choose this type of contract, because it meets their private and family interests at the same time as enabling them to participate in gainful employment. Working part-time gives employees more flexibility and is compatible with the new attitude towards working life, called *"downshifting"*. The employees have more time for their families, hobbies and other important aspects of their lives, without losing contact with the world of employment.

Before the Act on Part-Time and Fixed-Term Employment (Teilzeit-und Befristungsgesetz – TzBfG) came into effect in 2001, employees had no right to claim for a reduction or prolongation of the working time that had been agreed on in the contract.

The parties bound by the labour contract were only allowed to modify their original working time agreement by mutual consent.

The new law - espcially Section 8 TzBfG - the so-called "right of part-time work", which allowed employees to shorten the working hours originally agreed on by contract, initially triggered a large-scale public debate.

In order to qualify for this new regulation, there are two conditions that must be fulfilled.

The employee must have been employed by the establishment for more than six months and the total number of employees in the company must be more than 15 (excluding apprentices). Under these conditions the employee has the right to claim for a reduction of his or her overall working hours, and also to request a new schedule for the reduced time. The employees are not obliged to give reasons for their request or to discuss their intentions with their employer.

The employee must apply for a reduction of the contractually agreed working time at least three months in advance, and must give the employer details of the required new scheduling of his or her reduced working hours.

According to Section 8 paragraph 4 of the Act on Part-Time and Fixed-Term Employment (TzBfG), the employer can only refuse the employee's request for reduced working time for *"operational reasons"*.

The term "operational reasons" is not legally defined. The reason must of course be objective. The employer cannot refuse to accept the employee's right to work part-time because of additional administrative work or other organizational tasks. Even the fact of having to engage an additional employee to compensate for the part-time absence of an employee does not qualify as an "operational reason", unless the employer can prove that no comparably trained employee is available for the company on the labour market.

According to Section 8 paragraph 3 TzBfG, the parties of the labour contract must discuss the application for reduced working time and the new time schedule involved. If they cannot come to an agreement about both items, the employer has to reject the employee's request at least one month before the proposed changes. If the employer does not reject the employee's application in an appropriate manner and within reasonable time, the working time reduction will start, as requested, in accordance with the application and according to the wishes of the employee.

If the employer rejects the request of his employee without discussing with the employee any agreements about reduction and distribution of the new time schedule the working time reduciton will not start. The employee may repeat his or her request for reduced working time, but not before two years have passed.

If the employee does not accept the employer´s rejection, the employee must file a suit against the employer to the German Labour court. If there are no "operational reasons" to support the employer's point-blank refusal, the decision of the court will comply with the employee's request and replace the employers decision.

If the employer agrees to the requested reduction of working time and the new time schedule, the conditions of the working contract will change corresponding to the new agreement of the parties.

Objective operational reasons could include the following: if the reduced working hours seriously disturb the working process or the organisation of the company; if they cause unacceptibly high costs for the employer, or if the safety of the employees is affected to a significant degree.

The law also grants part-time employees the right to request an extension of their agreed working time, involving a longer part-time period, or even increasing it to full-time employment.

The right to reduce or to extend the working hours agreed on in the contract applies to all employees, whether they are full-time, part-time, temporary or fixed-term employees.

IV.   Contract for temporary Labour

A temporary employment agency recruits employees in order to hire them out to companies where they are regularly employed as "temp workers".

A temporary employment agency which commercially hires out employees to other companies needs a special licence or permission from the authorities.

Temporary employment is regulated by the Temporary Employment Act (Arbeitnehmerüberlassungsgesetz – AÜG) and is known informally as "time work" or "personal leasing".

There are two contractual relationships between these three parties, or the "triangle", as it is often referred to, meaning the temporary employment agency, the temporary employee and the company hiring the temp worker.

The temporary employee has a regular employment contract with the temporary employment agency, which can be cancelled only according to German Labour law and the German Act of Protection against Unlawful Dismissal (Kündigungsschutzgesetz KSchG). In the employment contract, the parties agree that the employee will be hired out permantly to other companies.

There is also a contractual relationship between the temporary employment agency and the company hiring the temp worker, concerning the conditions involved in the leasing of the employee.

However, there is no privity of contract between the temp worker and the company the employee is actually working for.

The temporary employee receives his wages from his contracting partner – the temporary employment agency - and not from the company where the employee is actually working. The temporary employment agency exercises the employer's rights according to the employment contract, for example in issuing a warning. Only the right of direction is transferred to the user enterprise.

If the temporary employment agency has no legal permission or has lost its licence, the contractual relationship between the employment agency and the employee is or becomes null and void.

In order to protect the temporary employee for this eventuaulity, Section 10 of the Temporary Employment Act (Arbeitnehmerüberlassungsgesetz – AÜG) stipulates an employment contract between the employee and the company which has hired the temp worker. It is only in this particular case that the law establishes privity of contract between the temporary employee and the company he is working for.

Temporary employees very often earn less than comparable employees working for the same company, but who have signed an employment contract with the company itself. According to Section 10 of the Temporary Employment Act (Arbeitnehmerüberlassungsgesetz – AÜG), the temporary agency has to provide equal working conditions, including the amount of the employee´s wages.

On the other hand, the temporary employment agency bills the user company a higher wage per hour than the temporary employee actually receives from the temporary agency as hourly payments.

According to a collective agreement in 2008, temporary agencies are is not allowed to pay the temporary workers less than the minimum wage. This is seen as the weakst part of this kind of employment relationship.

Because of the present high unemployment rate, the number of temporary employment contracts has been increasing continuously. People seeking employment often sign labour contracts with temporary employment agencies in the hope of obtaining a permanent job in the company they are leased to. German trade unions in particular regard the increase in temporary employment as an instrument used to further rationalization, with negative effects on the whole of the working world.

Each party within this triangle has different motives. For the employee, working for a temporary agency is a way to avoid unemployment and to gain professional work experience while improving his or her prospects of getting a full-time contract for an indefinite period.

The enterprise hiring the temp worker has the advantage of flexibility, being able to adjust its personnel to its current work and order situation. Even in times of full order books, enterprises often only increase their staff by hiring temporary employees. In difficult times, the company can cancel the contract with the temporary agency without regarding the provisions of the German Labour law. Their own core group of workers can remain intact.

If a temporary employee falls ill, sickness benefits are paid by the agency instead of the user company.

Furthermore, the the temporary agency is obliged to find a replacement for the sick worker, thus saving the company all the organizational effort involved.

V.   Contract for Marginal Employment / "mini-jobs"

The definition of marginal work is basically stipulated in section 8 of the German Social Security Act (Sozialgesetzbuch Teil 4 – SGB IV). The German law on statutory social insurance distinguishes between two kinds of marginal part-time work. On the one hand there is the "mini-jobber" who can earn up to 450.- € a month, and on the other hand the "midi-jobber", who can earn a maximum of 800.- € a month. Both types of marginal work have a different effect on income tax and on social insurance contributions.

The act mentioned above only defines the meaning of the term 'marginal work', while the working conditions and the rights and duties of the mini-jobbers and midi-jobbers are stipulated in German labour law.

According to Section 8, paragraph 1, number 1, of the German Social Security Act (Sozialgesetzbuch Teil 4 – SGB IV), if the monthly wage is 450,-- € or less, the employee is a so-called *"mini-jobber"* and excluded from paying income tax and social insurance contributions. It is only the maximum wage (450,-- € per month) that is of significance for the qualification as a "mini-job", regardless of the amount of weekly working hours. If the mini-jobber works as a marginal part-time worker for several employers, his or her total income is not allowed to amount to more than 450,-- € a month. Otherwise each employment relationship is liable to social insurance contributions and income tax payments.

Persons employed in a mini-job, with a maximum income of 450,-- € a month, are excluded from the statutory social security system. Nevertheless, the employer has to pay social security contributions for the mini-jobber. The employer pays 30 % of the wages to the statutory health insurance and to the German statutory pension insurance scheme. The employee himself pays neither statutory social security contributions nor income tax. On the other hand, the employee is not entitled to benefits from social security, in spite of the fact that his employer pays a fixed contribution into the system. This payment is considered to be a "flat-rate" contribution to the social security system in general, and is called "risk structure compensation".

According to Section 8, paragraph 1, number 2, SGB IV, persons only employed for a short period are also considered to be mini-jobbers, provided the employee only works for two months running in one year, or else for 50 days distributed over the year.

This exemption from the statutory social security system makes marginal part-time work, especially as a mini-jobber, a popular working relationship for married women and house-wives, who want to earn some extra money without paying taxes or social security contributions. Most mini-jobbers are protected by the social benefits of the employment relation-ships of their husbands.

The second kind of marginal part-time work is a so-called "midi-job", where the employee has a monthly income of be-tween 450,-- € and 800,-- €. Unlike mini-jobbers, midi-jobbers are covered by statutory social security systems. The social security contribution rate depends of the income and in-creases progressively.

At the same time German Labour law guarantees marginal workers continued wage payments of up to six weeks in the case of sick leave, 24 days' paid holiday and a Christmas bonus. The amount of the payment is proportional to that of a full time worker.

VI.   Homework / Telework

People seeking more compatibility between their work and their private lives, such as young fathers or mothers who want to spend more time with their family, or employees hoping to reduce their commuting distance, often opt for homework or telework.

This development is not being fired by employers, who are generally afraid that homeworkers and teleworkers cannot be supervised sufficiently and that data protection issues will not be dealt adequately.

Even so, the amount of teleworkers has increased during the last 10 years. Most of these employees were not originally hired as teleworkers, but worked as "normal" employees in the companies and changed later to homework or telework by mutual agreement.

Home workers enjoy the full protection of labour law and must be treated in the same way as other employees working on the premises of the company.

The first legal regulations for homework were laid down on December 20th. 1911 as the "Hausarbeitsgesetz".

Homework was originally a kind of wagework. The working place was and is – according to the choice of the home-worker - either his own apartment or house or any chosen place. The employer provides the requirements for produc-tion, and the home worker is paid according to the amount of items he produces. Unlike other employees, home workers are not integrated into the working organisation of the com-pany and the employers have no managerial authority. The home worker is free to decide where, when and how much to work. Employers are obliged to pay full social security contri-butions for home workers.

The most popular form of homework nowadays, telework or "e-work", is a subcategory of homework. The employees work mostly in their home office using the internet, and are supported by a range of modern telecommunication devic-es.

Flexible or rotating telework is very widespread. This means that work is done partly on company premises and partly in the teleworker's home office. One workstation in the compa-ny can be used by several teleworkers, following a time schedule to prevent overlappig.

The classical teleworker only works at home. There is however only a small group of employees who choose this kind of homework, because of the fear of wearing, monotonous work and the risk of social isolation.

The so called "mobile teleworkers" work in different locations outside the enterprise, e.g. visiting customers at home or working in national or international satellite offices of the company.

"On site"- telework means that external consultants are working within the enterprise and are supported by the working organisation of the company. This is the only form of homework which is not completely protected by German labour law.

German Labour Law does not include any express provisions regarding telework. Several drafts have been submitted in recent years, but in the end the idea of drawing up special legal regulations has always been abandoned, because telework is only a small phenomenon within the working world. in spite of the role that it could play in helping employers to save expenses.

VII.   Employment/ On-Call Work

German Labour law deals with "work on request" in Section 12 of the Act on Part-Time Work and Fixed-Term Contracts (Teilzeitbefristungsgesetz - TzBfG).

Employer and employee agree that whether the employee works or not depends on the volume of work in the company. This means that the employer only calls the employee when there is a heavy workload. Hence the working contract only regulates the basic agreement of the wage per work unit, but not necessarily the scope of the work or the length of such a working period. However, "open-ended" working hours are – even in that case - unlawful according to the German Federal Labour Court. [58]

This type of employment enables the employer to react flexibly to the work volume. It is very popular in the hotel and catering sector, especially in fast-food chains. The employees, however, have the disadvantages of an irregular and insecure income and long, irregular working hours.

Employer and employee must come to an agreement about the total daily or weekly work duration. If the agreement is missing, the employer is obliged to employ the employee for a minimum of 10 hours a week or three hours a day. Furthermore, the employer has to tell the employee at least four days in advance when he will be expected to start working. Otherwise the employee has the right to refuse to do the work.

The employer has to pay the employee for the mimimum of working hours agreed on by the parties, even he cannot employ the employee during that time.

On-call work deviates from the principle of Section 615 of the German Civil Code (Bürgerliches Gesetzbuch – BGB), which stipulates that the employer is responsible for the economic and business risks involved.

On-call employment can´t mixed up with other working time models, like shift work, emergency service or overtime.

---

[58] BAG 5 AZR 810/07 – 09.07.2008

Basics of German Labour Law
The Employment Relationship

VIII. Job-Sharing

In this employment model, the employer and several employees agree for two or more employees to share working time and one workplace. It is up to the members of the group to determine the working time of each job-sharer.

The basic form is "job-splitting". The working hours and the tasks of one full-time workplace are equally divided between the employees involved in the scheme.

Each employee has his or her own labour contract with the employer. The termination of one employment contract can thus never justify the dismissal of the other employees involved in the job-sharing group.

"Job-pairing" is a different kind of job-sharing, in which the participants and their work are dependent on each other. In this case, because the work of every member is connected to the work of the other job-sharers of the group, the sharing partners have to synchronise their work.

Unlike the basic form, the labour contracts of job-pairing group-members can only be terminated together, with one declaration of notice.

"Top-sharing" is a leadership model based on partnership. The members have equal responsibility and take important decisions together.

All types of job-sharing are, by definition, a kind of part-time work, and stipulated in Section 12 and 13 of the Act on Part-Time Work and Fixed-Term Contracts (Teilzeitbefristungsgesetz - TzBfG).

The cornerstone of job-sharing is replacement in case of illness or during vacation. If one of the job-sharers is unable to work, the other group-members are only obliged to replace the missing part if they have agreed to do so in every individual case, or if this obligation is included the employment contract.

This type of employment was initially introduced in the United States in the mid-eighties, but is seldom used in Germany.

Title VI
Jurisdiction

Chapter I
System of Labour Courts

The German jurisdiction has five jurisdictions of equal rank. These are the jurisdiction of the ordinary courts, the jurisdiction in labour matters, administrative jurisdiction, jurisdiction in social matters and the jurisdiction of the tax courts.

The German labour court system is three-tiered: The system starts with the Labour Court first instance (Arbeitsgericht), followed by the District Court (Landesarbeitsgericht) and on to the German Ferderal Labour Court (Bundesarbeitsgericht) in Erfurt.

According to Section 16 and the following section of the German Labour Court Law (Arbeitgerichtgesetz – ArbGG), the panel of the Labour Court of first instance is composed of a professional judge and two honorary judges, representing the employer and the employee respectively.

While the Labour Court of first instance and the District Labour Court - as second instance - are composed of one professional judge and two lay judges, the senates of the German Federal Labour Court consist of three professional judges and two lay judges, representing the employer and the employee respectively.

Chapter II
Organs of Judicature

I. Professional Judge

A professional judge is appointed according to the regulations of the German Judiciary Act (Deutsches Richtergesetz) and by the Minster of Labour and Social Affairs. He must have studied law at university and completed his studies after the first and second State Examinations. After three years of service the professional judge is appointed for an unlimited period of time and can only be recalled under specific circumstances. He is employed by the Federal State. Persuant to Section 42 of the German Labour Court Act (Arbeitsgerichtsgesetz – ArbGG), a professional judge of the Federal Court must be at least 35 years old. In courts of lower instance the age of the labour judge is not decisive.

Persuant to Article 97 of the German Constitution (Grundgesetz – GG), the judge is bound only by law and justice. Personal beliefs and motives may not influence his or her verdict. In case of commiting a breach of neutrality or in case of bias the judge can be suspended from his function.

II. Lay Judge

Lay judges are independent and not bound by instructions or court orders. They are appointed for the term of five years by the Minster of Labour and Social Affairs of the relevant federal state ("Land"). According to Section 21 of the German Labour Court Law, lay judges on the bench of Labour Courts of first instance must be at least 25 years old.

Honorary judges are supposed to have a certain insight into problems with employment relationships. Lay Judges representing the employee are normally nominated by trade unions, whereas the employer usually sends members of the employers' association to represent their interests in court.

A lay judge's vote carries as much weight as that of a professional judge. However, it rarely happens that the lay judges of the Labour Court of first instance and of the District Labour Court actually overrule the professional judge. In practice, the lay judge is expected to represent common sense as opposed to the professionalism of a trained judge.

3. Lawyers and other Representatives

The lawyers are also an organ of the judisdiction and they have the same training and take the same examinations as a professional judge. On the one hand the lawyer is the representative of his client, who can be either the employer or the employee, and on the other hand the lawyer is an independent agent of judicature and part of the institution of legal system.

In the Labour Court of first instance the employer and the employee can represent themselves, but in practice lawyers usually act on behalf of their clients. Furthermore, in the Labour Court of first instance legal aid representatives from the trade unions or representatives of employers' associations are allowed to represent the litigants.

While representation by a lawyer is not obligatory in Labour Courts of first instance, it is required on higher levels. According to Section 11 of the German Labour Court Act (Arbeitgerichtsgesetz – ArbGG), representation by an attorney is mandatory in cases before the Federal Labour Court.

Chapter III
Procedural Principles

I.   Venue and subject-matter jurisdiction

According to Section 48 of the German Labour Court Act (Arbeitsgerichtsgestz), the local jurisdiction of the court is determined either by the workplace of the employee or by the registered office of the employer or company. As stated in Section 2 of the German Labour Court Act (Arbeitsgerichtsgesetz), the Labour Courts have jurisdiction over all disputes arising from the employment relationship between employees and employers. Persuant to Section 2 and 2a of the German Labour Court Act (ArbGG), the Labour Courts have exclusive jurisdiction, meaning that the case cannot not be presented or heard before another court.

If a case is presented to a court that has not the competent jurisdiction, for example if an employee sues his employer for unfair dismissal before an ordinary court of law, the latter will transfer the lawsuit to the Labour Court.

II.   Procedure

The proceedings in the Labour Court follow the same rules as in an ordinary court of law.

Every court hearing in the Labour Court starts with a conciliation hearing, pursuant to Section 54 of the German Labour Court Act (ArbGG). The chairman – without the lay judges - discuss the whole dispute with the parties involved, regarding the facts, the legal issues and the evidence which has been presented. The purpose of the conciliation hearing is to find a compromise.

As laid down in Section 61 paragraph 2 of the German Labour Court Act (ArbGG), the hearing must take place within two weeks of the filing of the suit. If the parties cannot agree on a settlement, the judge will determine a date for an adversarial hearing before the entire panel. Within this period the parties must make their statements of defence. The judge normally requests the conflicting parties to attend the adversarial hearing in person.

The main procedural principles are: the principle of public trial, the principle of immediacy, the principle of oral proceedings, the principle of party presentation, the principle of party disposition, the principle of judicial investigation and the principle of concentration.

Time is an important factor in labour cases. The accerlation of the proceeding is stated in Section 9 of the German Labour Court Act (ArbGG), so the deadlines for replying to statements of the opponent are shorter than in ordinary civil proceedings.

III.   Appeal

The District Labour Court, as a court of second instance, is responsible for appeals against the decisions of the Labour Court of first instance, and examines the sentences on points of law and on points of fact, while the German Federal Labour Court reviews the sentences of the District Court only on points of law.

An appeal to the District Court is possible if the grievance is valued at more than 600.- € or if permission to appeal has been given explicitly. The parties are allowed to appeal against a sentence of the District Labour Court if the dispute is of fundamental importance, or if the District Court pronounces a judgement which diverges from the majority ruling of the Federal Labour Court.

IV.   Costs

The defeated party has to pay the court fees, which are very low, pursuant to the Court Fees Act (Gerichtskostengesetz).

In the first instance, on the other hand, every party has to pay the cost of its legal representative, so that even the winning party is obliged to pay the fees of its own lawyer.

The idea behind this is to minimize the employee´s risk of having to bear the costs of the employer's lawyer, which would prevent employees seeking legal help by invoking the labour court.

In the second and third instances, however, as in ordinary civil proceedings, the defeated party has to pay the court fees and the lawyers' fees of both plaintiff and defendant. If the employee cannot pay the costs of the proceedings without endangering his livelihood, he may apply for legal aid. If the other party – usually the employer – is represented by a lawyer, the employee can request to be assigned a lawyer, as stated in Section 11 a of the German Labour Court Act (ArbGG).

Chapter IV
Everyday Business at Court

As the statistics show, it is mostly employees or work councils that appeal to the Labour Court, and more than one third of the disputes between employees and employers are settled in the consiliation hearing. The most frequent cases are claims against unfair dismissal, claims for compensation after dismissal and disputes about employment references.

I.   Indemnity

In cases of unfair dismissal the conciliation hearing very often ends with a severance payment.

The main subject of controversy is the amount the employer has to pay his former employee. The last monthly wage and the duration of employment have a determining influence on the level of indemnity. There is a rule of thumb for calculating the amount due : the plaintiff can claim half of his last gross monthly wage per service year.

With the mediation of the Labour Court, the compensation settlement often combines different issues to soften the impact of the employee's job loss. The parties might, for example, change a termination without notice into a termination with notice, in order to forestall a reduction in his unemployment benefits, and embellish the settlement with a favourable reference. Employers often demand a non-disclosure agreement, in order to prevent the content of the settlement from being known within the company.

II.   Employment References

Every employee has the right to ask for an employment certificate, which must be issued on the day when the contract is terminated.

A distinction is made between an simple reference, which refers only to the type and duration of the employee's activity in the company, and a qualified reference, which also contains details of performance and conduct.

An employer is duty-bound to provide a job reference, but on other hand the employee has no right to demand particular wording in his reference. The content of the job reference must be genuine and favourable.

Certain expressions within a reference often give rise to suspicion, implying a secret code or language behind apparently favourable wording. Hence proceedings to rectify job references are part of everyday business at the Labour Court.

The following are examples of adjectives that can be used to express approval of a employee's work performance: "exceptional, outstanding, superior". "Dedicated and intelligent," for example, can be used to describe his character .The following phrases, *for example,* are clearly ambigious: *"You will be lucky to get him to work for you"* or " *"He was attentive to details, independent and flexible".*

The omission of a concluding sentence in the employer`s reference, saying, for example, that his former employer would be pleased to reemploy him, or the lack of a recommendation to any future employers, are interpreted in the light of this secret code and are everyday issues at Labour Courts. It goes without saying that employers deny the existence of any such code language in job references.

Basics of German Labour Law
The Employment Relationship

Private Notes